Essential Elements of

Management Accounting

Jill & Roger Hussey

Jill Hussey is an author and editor who specialises in management and business studies texts. Her writing reflects her recent experience as a mature student which has given her considerable insight into students' needs.

Roger Hussey is NWIS Professor of Financial Services at the University of the West of England, Bristol, and has wide experience in industry, research and teaching. He has written a number of books on accounting topics for students and practitioners.

Series adviser: Bob Cudmore BEd, MBA, Head of Management and Professional Studies Division, South Birmingham College

Technical adviser: David Holden BA (Hons), MSc, PGCE, South Birmingham College

Published in association with South Birmingham College
DP Publications Ltd
1994

Acknowledgements

We would like to thank the staff and students of the University of the West of England, Bristol, who over the years have enabled us to gain a wide experience of the teaching and learning needs of students.

A CIP catalogue reference for this book is available from the British Library

ISBN 1 85805 103 7

Typeset by Kai Typsetting, Nottingham

Printed in Great Britain by the Guernsey Press Co. Ltd, Vale, Guernsey

Preface

Aim

The aim of the *Essential Elements* series is to provide course support material covering the main subject areas of HND/C Business Studies and equivalent level courses at a price that students can afford. Students can select titles to suit the requirements of their own particular courses whether BTEC Certificate in Business Administration, Certificate in Marketing, IPS Foundation, Institute of Bankers, Access to Business Studies, Institute of Personnel Management, or other appropriate undergraduate and professional courses.

Many courses now have a modular structure, i.e. individual subjects are taught in a relatively short period of, say, 10 to 12 weeks. The *Essential Elements* series meets the need for material which can be built into the students' study programmes and used for directed self-study. All the texts, therefore, include activities with answers for students' self-assessment, activities for lecturer-assessment, and references to further reading.

The series is a joint venture between DP Publications and South Birmingham College.

How to use the series

All the books in the series are intended to be used as workbooks and provide approximately 70 hours of study material. Each text covers the essential elements of that subject, so that the core of any course at this level is covered, leaving the lecturer to add supplementary material if required. All have the following features:

❏ **In-text activities,** which aim to promote understanding of the principles, and are set at frequent intervals in the text. The solutions add to the student's knowledge, as well as providing an introduction to the next learning point.

❏ **End of chapter exercises**, some of which are intended for self-assessment by the student (these have solutions at the back of the book). Others are suitable for setting by the lecturer and answers or marking guides are provided in the Lecturers' Supplement. These exercises include progress and review questions, multiple choice questions, which test specific knowledge and allow rapid marking, practice questions, questions for advanced students, and assignments.

❏ **Further reading references** for students who wish to follow up particular topics in more depth.

❏ **Lecturers' Supplement**, which is available free of charge to lecturers adopting the book as a course text. It includes answers or guides to marking to help with student assessment.

Other titles in the series

Available 1994: Business Economics, Business Statistics, Business Planning and Policy, Financial Accounting, Marketing, Quantitative Methods.

Available 1995: Business Law, Human Resource Management, Management Information Systems, Operations Management.

Contents

1 The role of management accounting

1.1 Introduction

This chapter introduces and describes the main forms of accounting. It identifies the roles of financial and management accountants and some of the alternative titles which may be used. It also examines the importance of financial information to managers and the value of management accounting to an organisation.

On completing this chapter you should be able to:

❐ describe what is meant by the term 'accounting';

❐ differentiate between financial accounting and management accounting;

❐ explain the role of the management accountant;

❐ describe the purpose and value of management accounting.

1.2 Definition of accounting

In its broadest form, *accounting* is concerned with identifying, measuring, recording and communicating the economic transactions of organisations. It is useful to consider each of these activities separately.

❐ *Identifying* economic transactions in most instances is fairly straightforward. Examples include selling goods to customers, paying wages, purchasing new stock, buying machinery or equipment.

❐ *Measuring* economic transactions is carried out using money as the form of measurement. Instead of saying that we have sold 20 kilos of tomatoes, we say that we have sold 20 kilos of tomatoes at 30p per kilo. Therefore the total sale is £6.

❐ *Recording* the economic transactions is essential. They may be recorded in hand-written books of accounts or on suitable computer software.

❐ *Communicating* the economic transactions is done by producing financial statements. The two main forms of financial statement for external purposes are the *profit and loss account* and the *balance sheet*. However, organisations prepare a number of financial statements for internal purposes.

Activity

A business buys 5 litres of paint, 20 metres of timber and employs a carpenter for two days to build shelves in an office. If paint costs £4 per litre, timber costs £2.50 per metre and the carpenter charges £50 per day, what is the total cost of the shelves?

In answering this question you will have been carrying out the basic accounting procedure of identifying, measuring and recording in monetary terms the building of the office shelves. The cost can be calculated in a number of stages. First you may have decided to multiply the cost of paint per litre by the amount used. Next, you may have multiplied the cost of timber per metre by the amount used. Finally, you may have calculated the cost of employing the carpenter by multiplying his daily rate by the number of days. It does not matter in which order you decided to work out the figures, as long as you arrived at three figures which when added together make up the total cost of the job. The correct figures are as follows:

Cost statement for two shelves

	£
Cost of paint (£4 x 5 litres)	20
Cost of timber (£2.50 x 20 metres)	50
Cost of labour (£50 x 2 days)	100
Total cost of the shelves	170

The above financial statement provides a record of a number of transactions and the information is useful for deciding whether to have the work done or, it has been already been done, for finding out how the total cost was calculated.

Although in this section we have looked at accounting in its broadest form, the subject can be divided into *financial accounting* and *management accounting*. In this chapter we shall start by looking briefly at financial accounting, but the remainder of the chapter will be concerned with management accounting.

1.3 Financial accounting

Financial accounting is concerned with the classification, measurement and recording of business transactions. After a specified period of time, normally a year but possibly more frequently, the information is communication by means of *financial statements*. The main financial statements are the *profit and loss account* and the *balance sheet*. These two financial statements are prepared for the benefit of the owner(s) of the business, although others may also be interested in them

Financial accounting aims to present a *true and fair view* of business transactions and is conducted within a *regulatory framework*. This means that there are certain legal and other obligations which different organisations must adhere to. It is based on *assumptions* which have been established as general principles. Financial accounting can be divided into a number of specific activities such as the following:

❑ *bookkeeping*, which is concerned with recording business transactions;

❑ *auditing*, which is the thorough examination of the financial records of an organisation to confirm that the financial statements give a true and fair view (an audit is legally required for limited companies);

❑ *corporate recovery*, which is an increasingly important area of accounting and covers the provision of insolvency services and advice to companies in financial difficulty;

❑ *taxation advice*, which is governed by legislation and involves individuals and businesses.

Activity

Select the correct response to the following statements:

		True	False

A financial accountant can give advice on the following matters:

i)   How to arrange financial affairs so that the least amount of tax is incurred.

ii) The best way to borrow money for a specific project.

iii) The cost of launching a new product or service.

iv) The financial benefits of introducing new technology.

v)   The cost of a pay offer to be put to the workforce.

vi) The likely profit to be made on a huge rock concert.

You may have been puzzled by some of these statements, but you would be right if you said that they are all the concern of the accountant. Wherever there is a need for financial information, the accountant plays an important role. In some organisations the roles of financial and management accountants overlap or may be combined. Therefore, it is not possible to say with certainty who would deal with the above matters in specific organisations. Normally i), ii), and vi) would fall within the expertise of a financial accountant and iii), iv) and v) are the domain of the management accountant.

1.4 Management accounting

Management accounting uses a range of financial and statistical techniques and methods to provide information to managers. A management accountant is concerned with identifying why the information is required so that the most appropriate technique can be used to supply information to managers which will be of value. Management needs this information to enable them to *plan* the progress of the business, *control* the activities and see the financial implications of any *decisions* they may take. Unlike financial accounting, management accounting is not governed by legislation or other regulations.

To illustrate the difference between financial accounting and management accounting we can look back at the example of the office shelves. A financial accountant would be interested in the total cost of £170 so that it can be recorded as the economic transaction. A management accountant would be more concerned with informing managers how much the individual elements (the paint, timber and labour) cost. A management accountant would also want to calculate how much the shelves actually cost and compare it with a plan or budget of what it was estimated they would cost. In setting the plan, a management accountant would also want to look at a number of different ways and costs involved in building the shelves so that management can decide which is the preferred way.

Activity

Classify the following activities into financial accounting and management accounting.

	Financial accounting	Management accounting

i) Auditing the books of an organisation.

ii) Managing an organisation's tax affairs.

iii) Analysing the financial implications of management decisions.

iv) Preparing the financial statements at the year end.

v) Ensuring compliance with legal and other regulations.

vi) Providing financial information for managers.

vii) Keeping the financial records of an organisation.

By now you are probably more confident about deciding which activities involve financial accounting and which can be classified as management accounting. With the exception of iii) and vi), the above activities are concerned with financial accounting.

1.5 The management accountant

Not all organisations employ a management accountant. In a very small business the owner may keep the financial records and employ a firm of accountants to draw up the financial statements and sort out tax matters at the year end. In larger organisations an accountant is more likely to be employed.

Activity

If an organisation employs only one accountant, do you think his or her time will be mainly spent carrying out tasks which fall into the domain of:

i) Management accounting

ii) Financial accounting

iii) Both management and financial accounting

iv) Neither management nor financial accounting

Answer iv) is obviously wrong because there is no point in employing an accountant who does not carry out any accounting tasks at all. Which of the other answers is right may not be obvious until you remember that by law most organisations must produce financial statements; this task is carried out by a financial accountant. However, if the accountant has time, he or she will also undertake management accounting. Therefore, both answers ii) and iii) could be right. If only one accountant is employed, it would be very unusual if most of his or her time is spent carrying out management accounting tasks. However, depending on the type of organisation and the use made of outside consultants, it is not impossible. So answer i) might be correct in certain circumstances.

In large organisations it is normal to employ some staff who specialise in financial accounting and some who specialise in management accounting. Other titles sometimes used for a management accountant are *operations accountant, planning accountant, strategic accountant, factory accountant, project accountant* or *budget accountant*. In some cases the accountant may be concerned with only one part of the management accounting function. Some organisations have developed their own titles or use the above titles in unexpected ways, so the job title is not an accurate guide. A slightly old fashioned title which is still in use, particularly in certain industries, is that of *cost accountant*. It denotes that the person has specific responsibilities for that part of management accounting which is concerned with collecting and analysing costs.

If you are trying to identify who is responsible for management accounting in an organisation, you could also try looking at the work produced. If the accountant publishes detailed financial information on a frequent basis for internal use, it is most likely that he or she is a management accountant.

Management accountants are often members of a professional accountancy body, usually the Chartered Institute of Management Accountants (CIMA). A member of CIMA will have trained as an accountant in industry and passed a number of rigorous examinations. He or she is entitled to use the letters ACMA or FCMA after his or her name.

1.6 The purpose and value of management accounting

The *purpose* of management accounting is to provide managers with financial and statistical information which will help them carry out their responsibilities. The responsibilities of managers in any organisation can be classified as *planning, controlling* and *decision making*. Therefore the financial information they require should help them to control the resources for which they are responsible, plan how those resources can be most effectively used and decide what course of action they should take when a number of options are open.

Activity

Imagine you are a manager and indicate whether you would require the following information for planning, controlling or decision-making.

	Planning	Controlling	Decision making
i) The amount claimed for taxi fares by staff last month.			
ii) The prices charged by a new supplier for materials.			
iii) The cost of running the office photocopier.			
iv) The cost of employing sub-contracted staff compared with using your own employees.			
v) The cost of making a component compared with buying it from an outside supplier.			

Items iv) and v) should be easy to define because in both circumstances you are choosing between alternatives and are therefore making decisions. With items i) and iii) you are mainly concerned with controlling costs, although you might want the information to make plans for future expenditure. Item ii) could be concerned with planning future costs or you may be about to decide whether to change to another supplier. This decision may have arisen because you are trying to control costs. Although the boundaries between planning, controlling and decision-making are blurred, financial information has a very important role to play and it is the management accountant who provides this information.

Management accounting is concerned with providing financial information which is of *value* to managers. It therefore offers a number of general advantages, such as helping the organisation to be more profitable or, in a non-profit organisation, ensuring that it is providing value for money.

Activity

What other advantages do you consider a management accounting system offers to organisations? Draw up a list of the advantages under the headings of planning, controlling and decision-making.

Your list may include some of the following examples:

Planning

❏ the price of products or services;

❏ the number of employees that will be needed in the future and what they should be paid;

❏ the quantity of each product or service which must be sold to achieve a desired level of profit.

Controlling

❏ unnecessary expense and waste;

❏ the amount of investment made in plant and machinery;

❏ the cost of running different departments.

Deciding

❏ whether to make or buy a particular component;

❏ whether it is financially worthwhile investing in new technology;

❏ which products or services to offer if there is a shortage of skilled labour.

1.7 Summary

In this chapter we have looked at the two main divisions of accounting, financial and management accounting. You have discovered various methods which can be used to find out who is responsible for management accounting in an organisation. We have also examined the purposes and value of management accounting and how it helps managers to do their jobs.

Further reading

Dyson, J. R., *Accounting for Non-Accounting Students*, Pitman, 1991, Chapter 1.

Glautier, M. W. E. & Underdown, B., *Cost Accounting*, Pitman, 1988, Chapter 1.

Hussey, Roger, *Cost and Management Accounting*, Macmillan Professional Masters, 1989, Chapter 1.

Lucey, T., *Cost and Management Accounting*, DP Publications, 1992, Chapter 1.

Exercises

Progress questions

These questions have been designed to help you remember the key points in this chapter. The answers to these questions are given on page 94.

Complete the following sentences:

1. Accounting is concerned with ....

2. Financial accounting is concerned with ....

3. Management accounting is concerned with ....

4. A management accountant provides information to managers to help them with their responsibilities of ....

5. A qualified management accountant is normally a member of ....

....

Select the correct response to the following statements:

6. Financial accounting is concerned with such matters as stock levels, number of labour hours used in manufacturing, purchase of new equipment etc.

    True ☐ False ☐

7. The management accountant is the person primarily responsible for financial control.

    True ☐ False ☐

8. Companies are required by law to publish management accounts.

    True ☐ False ☐

9. A management accountant normally receives his or her training in industry.

    True ☐ False ☐

10. The main value of management accounting is the help it gives to managers.

    True ☐ False ☐

Review questions

These questions have been designed to help you check your comprehension of the key points in this chapter. You may wish to look further than the text in this chapter in order to answer them fully. You will find your library useful as a source of wider reading. You can check your answers by referring to the appropriate section.

11. Describe the key features of the definition of accounting. (Section 1.2)

12. What are the main differences between the activities of a financial accountant and those of a management accountant? (Sections 1.3 and 1.4)

13. What alternative titles can be used for a management accountant? (Section 1.5)

14. What are the benefits of management accounting? (Section 1.6)

Multiple choice questions

The answers to these questions will be given in the Lecturer's Supplement.

15. The two main forms of accounting are:
    a) bookkeeping and auditing
    b) taxation and investment appraisal
    c) financial and management accounting
    d) profit and loss account and balance sheet

16. Which of the following are normally the responsibility of a financial accountant:
    a) calculating liability for tax
    b) calculating the cost of a project
    c) identifying the financial implications of investing in alternative types of equipment
    d) keeping proper accounting records of transactions

17. A management accountant is normally most concerned with:
    a) ensuring that an organisation pays the correct amount of tax
    b) providing information that will be of use to managers
    c) auditing the books of an organisation
    d) keeping financial records of transactions

18. By law, a management accountant must be:
    a) a member of a professional accounting body
    b) a holder of a degree in accountancy
    c) authorised by the Department of Trade and Industry
    d) None of these

19. A management accountant is responsible for providing financial information
    a) every six months
    b) once a year
    c) whenever managers requires it to carry out their responsibilities
    d) only when a new product or service is being planned

Practice questions

> *A marking guide to these questions will be given in the Lecturer's Supplement.*

20. Explain the different roles of the financial and management accountants.

21. Explain how management accounting contributes to the other functions of management.

22. Describe the range of work a management accountant would be concerned with.

Questions for advanced students

> *A marking guide to these questions will be given in the Lecturer's Supplement.*

23. What are the advantages and disadvantages of management accounting information to a person outside the company?

24. Describe the main advantages of a management accounting system.

Assignment: Bouncy Enterprises Ltd

A marking guide to this assignment will be given in the Lecturer's Supplement.

For the last two years you have working as a financial accountant for Bouncy Enterprises Ltd which makes bouncy castles for children's play schemes. You are the only qualified accountant employed. Since the firm was established, four years ago, the business has expanded and you are now beginning too find the pressure of work too much. It occurs to you that it would be a good idea to recruit an assistant to take on the management accounting responsibilities.

Required

Write a report addressed to the managing director of Bouncy Enterprises giving details of your proposal. The main points you should address are:

i) The difference between financial and management accounting.

ii) The sort of work the management accountant would do.

iii) The type of qualifications and experience he or she should have.

iv) The value of management accounting to the business.

2 Cost classification and control

2.1 Introduction

This chapter introduces the idea of cost and describes the various classifications of cost and the reasons for using them in organisations. On completing this chapter you should be able to:

❏ explain what is meant by cost, cost units and cost centres;

❏ identify the cost units appropriate to different organisations;

❏ classify costs in a number of different ways;

❏ describe the procedure for costing for materials and labour.

2.2 Definition of cost

Before we start looking at what is meant by the term cost, it is useful to consider why cost is important in an organisation. The example we are going to use is that of a manufacturing company, but the reasons apply to all organisations.

Activity

Jot down three reasons why a manufacturing company might wish to know the costs of making its products.

The reasons you have listed may differ from those given below, depending on the assumptions you have made and your knowledge of manufacturing organisations. However, if you remembered from Chapter 1 that all organisations use financial information for planning, control and decision making, you will probably have identified the following reasons.

❏ *Establishing the selling price* - Unless a manufacturer knows the cost of making its products, it is not possible to decide on the selling price. If the market is very buoyant, the manufacturer may be able to charge a very high price, but it is still important to ensure that this covers the cost. If competition is very intensive, the manufacturer may wish to know how far the selling price of the product can be reduced before a loss is made.

❏ *Planning production* - It would be very difficult to determine the best way to plan production without knowing the relevant costs. It is necessary to know the costs of all the items making up the production process and the funds required to support them. Such costs are not confined to materials and labour, but also include machinery, buildings, transport, administration, maintenance and many other items.

❑ *Management control* - Managers have no control if they do not know the costs incurred and are unable to compare them with the original plan. This would lead to the resources used by the organisation being employed inefficiently, leading to waste, and in the worst circumstances to the complete failure of the organisation.

❑ *Decision making* - Managers are constantly making decisions and it is often imperative that they have knowledge of costs for the correct decisions to be taken. For example, it is impossible to decide whether it is worthwhile investing in new manufacturing machinery without having financial information.

Although it is important to know the costs, they are not always easy to identify. Let us take a simple example. You go to a high street computer dealer one Friday and buy a box of five floppy disks for £15. On Sunday your friend asks you to sell him one for some urgent work he is doing. You know that if you were to replace that disk on Monday it would cost you £3.50.

Activity

What do you think is the cost of the disk?
i) £3.00
ii) £3.50
iii) Both these figures
iv) Neither of these figures

You may have answered this by taking the original cost of 5 disks (£15) and dividing it by the number of disks to reach the answer of £3.00, or you have decided that the cost is Monday's price of £3.50. However, you may be surprised to know that in some senses all the answers are correct. But to know which is the most appropriate answer, we need to define the word cost precisely and put it in a context.

One difficulty is that our view of cost is determined by our different perspectives as buyers and sellers, the context in which we are making our calculations and the reasons for wanting this information. In addition, cost can be used as a verb, meaning to calculate the cost of a specified thing or activity; as a noun, meaning the amount of actual or notional expenditure incurred on or attributable to a specified thing or activity, or as an adjective.

2.3 Cost units and centres

The above definitions include the phrase 'a specified thing or activity'. All organisations provide an identifiable *output* which may be in the form of a service, product or both. The output of a business can be measured by devising some form of *cost unit*. A cost unit can be defined as a quantitative unit of the product or service to which costs are allocated. The type of cost unit depends on the type of industry. In a manufacturing industry there may be a large number of identical products. A brick works, for example, may have a cost unit of 1,000 bricks, because the cost of one brick is so small that it would be difficult to measure. In a service industry the cost unit may be of a more abstract nature. In a hospital, for example, the cost unit may be a patient-bed-occupied.

Some of these businesses may have been more difficult than others to find suitable cost units for, particularly if you are not familiar with the industries. However, you may have identified some of the following types of cost unit:

❑ A vehicle manufacturer would use a vehicle as a cost unit. If the same organisation manufactures the engine, gearbox, body and electrical system, these could also be treated as separate cost units.

❑ A carrier bag manufacturer has the same problems as a brick manufacturer: the costs identified with manufacturing one carrier bag are so small that they cannot be measured. Therefore a suitable cost unit would be 1,000 bags.

❑ A transport company is a bit more difficult. You need to consider what information the company would find useful. This might be the costs associated with moving one tonne of goods over one kilometre. Therefore, the cost unit will be one tonne kilometre.

❑ A plumber often works on a number of small jobs which may vary from fitting a bathroom suite to replacing a washer. The plumber needs to know the costs of each job and so a suitable cost unit would be each job.

❑ A ball point pen manufacturer as the same problem as the carrier bag manufacturer, the problem of size. Therefore an appropriate cost unit would be 1,000 pens.

❑ A small paint manufacturer producing specialist paints may choose a litre as the cost unit, but a large manufacturer may decide that a cost unit of 1,000 litre cans is sufficiently detailed to supply the information required.

As well as calculating the *costs* for each *cost unit*, an organisation may also need to know the costs for particular *cost centres*. A cost centre may be a single factory, a department or section, a single machine or group of machines, an individual or a group of individuals.

Activity

Tick which of the following might be cost centres in two examples below.

Harmonica manufacturer	Hotel
Assembly department	Kitchen
Stores department	Cost of drinks sold
Sales team	Reception area
Specialised moulding machine	Laundry
Clerical salaries	Restaurant

You may not know anything about the manufacture of harmonicas, but the definition of a cost centre given above should have helped you to identify the first four of these as possible cost centres. Clerical salaries are an expense, but not a cost centre. The specialised moulding machine may be a cost centre if it is sufficiently important and complex to allow a number of costs to be identified with that particular activity. Of course, not all harmonica manufacturers would use the above cost centres, but they are all areas of activity where managers may need to know the costs.

As far as the hotel is concerned, the cost of drinks sold is an item of expense, but all the others are possible cost centres.

Activity

Some organisations do not formally identify their cost centres and/or cost units. Answering the following questions may help you to identify the cost centres in your college or at work.

i) What are the cost centres and cost units in the organisation?

ii) What financial information is generated in respect of the cost centres and cost units?

iii) Do you have direct responsibility for any of them or are you able to influence them?

If you work in a manufacturing organisation, it should have been easy to identify the cost units as being the products made. In a service organisation or in a college, it would have been more difficult, as there may not be any identifiable cost units. In a hotel the cost unit used may be the room occupancy; in a distribution company a cost unit might be a tonne/mile (the cost involved in moving a tonne of goods one mile). In a college it may not be possible to identify any cost units.

You will have found it easier to identify cost centres as these are usually clearly defined. One example you may have given is that of a works canteen or a college refectory. Examples of the sort of financial information which would be available are staff wages, heating, lighting, food, etc. The meals may be used as the cost units. The degree of financial sophistication in the organisation determines whether they are treated as such.

2.4 Cost classification

Although it may be useful to know the total costs of an organisation for a financial period or the cost of one cost unit, it is even more useful if the costs are *classified*. By classifying costs we can obtain more detailed information and use it in a variety of ways for planning, controlling and decision-making. Classifying costs helps us to understand better what is meant by the term cost. The main classifications are:

- ❐ *direct costs*, which can be identified with a specific product or saleable service such as materials used in production, and *indirect costs*, which cannot be identified with any particular product or service but are shared, such as supervisors' salaries;

- ❐ *fixed costs*, which tend to remain the same in total irrespective of changes in the level of activity, and *variable costs*, which tend to change in total in direct proportion to changes in the level of activity;

- ❐ classification by the *nature* of costs (see Chapter 3), such as material, labour and expenses, which can be further divided into raw materials, maintenance materials, etc;

- ❐ classification by the *function* of costs, such as production, administration, selling and distribution costs.

Activity

Indicate which of the costs in the following list are normally classified as direct, indirect, fixed or variable costs in a manufacturing organisation.

	Direct costs	Indirect costs	Fixed costs	Variable costs
Materials used in the product				
Rent of the factory				
Insurance of the factory				
Depreciation				
Maintenance of machinery				
Canteen				
Supervisors' salaries				
Production workers' wages				
Accountants' salaries				

Even if you do not have any experience of working in a manufacturing environment, you should have been able to identify these from the definitions of direct and indirect costs. Materials and production workers' wages can be identified with the product and are therefore direct costs. Rent, insurance, maintenance of machinery, canteen, supervisors' salaries and accountants' salaries cannot be identified with any one particular product, but must be shared over a number of them. Therefore these are indirect costs.

You may have had more difficulty in distinguishing between fixed and variable costs and we shall be looking more closely at them in the next activity. One thing you may have noticed is that direct costs are always variable costs. For example, the materials used in the product can be directly identified with it and the more products made, the higher the total material costs will be. Therefore these are variable costs. In the above list the indirect costs are also all fixed costs, but in certain situations some indirect costs may be variable costs.

In the following example, the expenses of a taxi business have been broken down in some detail. This can be used as the basis for calculating further cost information.

Activity

Sam Reeve owns a taxi business. The average mileage by a taxi in one quarter is 15,000 miles and the costs, analysed by nature are as follows:

Expense	Total for quarter £
Driver's salary	2,670
Petrol and oil	1,050
Annual service	450
Taxation and insurance	1,110
Depreciation	870

What further useful information can you calculate from the above list of costs?

You will probably have realised that you can add up the costs so that Sam can find out that the total costs for one vehicle for one quarter are £6,150. From this you can then calculate the total cost per mile as:

$$\text{Total cost per mile} = \frac{\text{Total costs}}{\text{Total mileage}} = \frac{£6,150}{15,000} = 41\text{p per mile}$$

Having got this far, you can then work out the cost per mile for each of the expenses, as follows.

Expense	Total for quarter £	Cost per mile pence
Driver's salary	2,670	17.8
Petrol and oil	1,050	7.0
Annual service	450	3.0
Taxation and insurance	1,110	7.4
Depreciation	870	5.8
Total	6,150	41.0

Sam now has a considerable amount of information, including the total cost per unit (in this example a cost unit is one mile), and this total cost is further analysed by the nature of the expense. However, there are some dangers if Sam tries to use this cost information without understanding the difference between fixed and variable costs.

Activity

What is the cost per mile if the taxi travelled 30,000 miles in one quarter?

Your immediate response may have been to say that the cost per mile would remain at 41p. However, on consideration, you may have seen that the cost per mile is likely to be lower. This is because the *total fixed costs*, that is the cost of the driver's salary, taxation, insurance and depreciation, tend to remain the same, even though the mileage has doubled. On the other hand, the *total variable costs*, that is the cost of petrol and oil, tend to change in direct proportion to the change in the level of activity. This means that if activity, in our example, mileage, doubles, the variable costs will tend to double.

We shall be looking at the importance of fixed and variable costs again in Chapter 4, but for the moment you should remember that calculating the average cost per unit can be misleading if there are significant changes in the activity level of the business.

2.5 Elements of cost

The total cost of a product or service is built up from a number of elements of cost. The following diagram refers to a manufacturing organisation.

> *Direct materials*
> which become part of the finished goods

plus

> *Direct labour*
> which converts direct materials into the finished goods

plus

> *Direct expenses*
> such as subcontracted work or special tools

gives

> **Prime cost**

plus

> *Production overheads*
> which are the indirect costs
> arising from the provision of the production resources

gives

> **Production cost**

plus

> *Administration, sales and distribution overheads*
> which are the indirect costs analysed by function

gives

> **Total product cost**

A system is needed to charge the *direct materials, labour and expenses* to the cost unit. *Direct materials* may be charged to the cost unit by the production department using a materials requisition or stores issue note. These are documents which show the quantity and cost of the materials to be charged to the cost units. These documents are passed to the accounts department which maintains the costing records. The direct materials become part of the finished goods. *Direct labour* converts the direct materials into the finished goods. The time spent on cost units may be calculated from time sheets, job cards or computerised records. *Direct expenses* are not always present. They may include such items as subcontract work, or special tools or equipment bought for a particular job. The accounts department may use the invoices to charge the cost to the appropriate cost units.

Production overheads are those indirect costs which arise from the provision of the production resources. Examples include factory rent and rates, factory insurance, canteen costs. *Administration overheads* are those indirect costs which arise from the provision of the administrative function. *Sales overheads* are those indirect costs which arise from the sale of the cost unit. Examples include advertising and the salaries of the sales force. *Distribution overheads* are those indirect costs arising from the activity of getting the cost unit to the customer, such as packing and transport costs.

Activity

Select any well-known household item and describe the various elements of cost which may have been incurred in arriving at the total cost.

Even if you have selected a simple item you will be surprised by how complex the activities involved in its manufacture are, and therefore how difficult it is to ascertain the elements of cost. For example, in the case of a small business bottling spring water, the following elements may be found:

Direct materials:
  Plastic bottles and lids
  Water
  Labels

Direct labour:
  Bottling plant wages

Production overheads:
  Factory rent and rates
  Heat, light and power
  Depreciation of machinery
  Supervisors' salaries
  Maintenance and cleaners' wages
  Packaging materials

Selling and administration overheads

In our example, direct materials and direct labour have to be identified with each individual cost unit. To do this, the business needs good procedures for controlling and recording the costs.

2.6 Costing for materials

Materials represent a substantial cost in many businesses. The procedure for *costing for materials* should ensure that:

❐ the correct materials are delivered;

❐ materials are correctly stored and issued only with proper authorisation;

❐ production is charged with the cost of materials used;

❐ stored materials are correctly valued.

The main stages in costing for materials are:

1. A purchase requisition is sent to the buyer by the production department or stores department specifying the type and quantity of materials required.

2. The buyer sends a purchase order to the supplier.

3. The supplier sends the materials with a goods received note (GRN). The GRN is checked against the materials received and compared with the original order.

4. The materials are taken to the stores department and added to the stock. The quantity is added to the stock level shown on the bin card.

5. The production department requiring the materials sends a materials requisition note to the stores department. The stores department issues the materials and deducts the quantity from the stock level shown on the bin card.

Although adequate records may be maintained, proper control is exercised through a physical examination and count of materials in store known as *stock-taking*. This may be periodic or continuous. In a perpetual inventory system, a stores record card is maintained to give the quantity of each item in store as a balance after each issue and receipt has been physically checked.

Activity

Draw a diagram showing the flow of documents used to control the movement of materials.

The design of your diagram will depend on your creative abilities and the assumptions you have made, but you should have shown a logical flow of information. One thing to bear in mind is that copies of the documents will be sent to the accounts department so that they can ensure that goods have been properly ordered and received before paying the supplier's invoice. The accounts department also maintains costing records so that it is possible to calculate the cost of a unit.

2.7 Pricing materials issues

Having looked at the procedures and documents for purchasing, storing and issuing materials to production, we now need to consider the price at which they are issued from stores. This is more complex than it first appears. The materials in store will normally have been received on different dates and perhaps at a number of different purchase prices. It may be impossible to identify each issue of materials to production with the corresponding receipt into stores.

The main methods are:

❒ *first in, first out (FIFO)*, which uses the price of the first delivery of materials for all issues from store until that particular consignment has been exhausted, followed by the price of the subsequent consignment;

❒ *last in, first out (LIFO)*, which uses the price of the last delivery of materials for all issues from store until that particular consignment has been exhausted, followed by the price of the previous consignment;

❒ *average price method*, which uses either a simple average or a weighted average price for all issues from store;

❏ *replacement price method*, which uses the replacement price on the day of issue to value materials issued from store;

❏ *standard price method*, which uses a predetermined standard price for all issues and returns of materials from store.

Activity

A stores department has a record of the following receipts and issues of materials:

1st January received 1,000 kilos of materials at £2.00 per kilo

2nd January received 1,000 kilos of materials at £2.20 per kilo

3rd January issued 500 kilos to production

Calculate the cost of the 500 kilos of stock issued to production using as many different methods as possible.

From the information given, you could only use the first three methods described. Therefore, your answer should be:

500 kilos at £2.00 per kilo is £1,000 (using FIFO)

500 kilos at £2.20 per kilo is £1,100 (using LIFO)

500 kilos at £2.10 per kilo is £1,050 (using average price)

As you can see, the cost of materials used in production varies according to the method used. All these methods are correct and other methods which organisations use may also be acceptable. Each method has advantages and disadvantages. Of the three described above, FIFO makes sense in that most organisations tend to issue from stores the materials they had first received. This method is also acceptable to accountants and the Inland Revenue, whereas LIFO is not recommended by accountants and is not normally acceptable to the Inland Revenue.

The method used to price the issues of materials from stores also determines the value of the materials remaining in the stores. In some organisations the value of materials remaining in stores is very high. The materials must be kept safe and secure, and in a position where they can be issued conveniently to production. Records should be maintained of the quantity of goods in store at any one time. Because of the possibility of errors and theft, it is essential that a physical count of items in store is taken at regular intervals. Some organisations carry out *periodic stock-taking* with a physical count of all materials at a given date. This is done at least annually and requires a substantial amount of work and organisation. It can be very disruptive. Some organisations use *continuous stock-taking* where staff are employed to check a few items every day so that all stock is checked at least once a year. Whichever method of counting the physical quantity is used, the method used for pricing the issue of materials affects the value of the materials remaining in store.

Activity

Calculate the value of the remaining 1,500 kilos of materials in stock using the three methods, FIFO, LIFO and average price.

You should have calculated the value of the remaining 1,500 kilos as follows:

FIFO   £

Receipts:

1st January	1,000 kilos at £2.00 per kilo	2,000
2nd January	1,000 kilos at £2.20 per kilo	2,200
Total stock	2,000 kilos	4,200

Issues of materials:

| 3rd January | 500 kilos at £2.00 | 1,000 |
| Value of remaining stock | (1,500 kilos) | 3,200 |

LIFO   £

Receipts:

1st January	1,000 kilos at £2.00 per kilo	2,000
2nd January	1,000 kilos at £2.20 per kilo	2,200
Total stock	2,000 kilos	4,200

Issues of materials:

| 3rd January | 500 kilos at £2.20 | 1,100 |
| Value of remaining stock | (1,500 kilos) | 3,100 |

Average price   £

Receipts:

1st January	1,000 kilos at £2.00 per kilo	2,000
2nd January	1,000 kilos at £2.20 per kilo	2,200
Total stock	2,000 kilos	4,200

Issues of materials:

| 3rd January | 500 kilos at £2.10 | 1,050 |
| Value of remaining stock | (1,500 kilos) | 3,150 |

Once again, all these values are correct, depending on the method the organisation uses. It is clearly important for the organisation to use the same method consistently and not change it unless there is a very good reason.

Activity

To make certain that you understand the three methods, we will use the information above but add to it. Let us imagine that on the 4th January a further 600 kilos of materials are issued from stores. Using the three different methods, what is the cost of the materials issued to production and what is the value of the stock remaining in store?

You should not have had too much difficulty with this. The correct answer is shown on the following page.

FIFO £

Receipts:

1st January	1,000 kilos at £2.00 per kilo	2,000
2nd January	1,000 kilos at £2.20 per kilo	2,200
Total stock	2,000 kilos	4,200

Issues of materials:

3rd January	500 kilos at £2.00	1,000
Value of remaining stock	(1,500 kilos)	3,200

Issues of materials:

4th January	500 kilos at £2.00	
	100 kilos at £2.20	1,220
Value of remaining stock	(900 kilos)	1,980

LIFO £

Receipts:

1st January	1,000 kilos at £2.00 per kilo	2,000
2nd January	1,000 kilos at £2.20 per kilo	2,200
Total stock	2,000 kilos	4,200

Issues of materials:

3rd January	500 kilos at £2.20	1,100
Value of remaining stock	(1,500 kilos)	3,100

Issues of materials:

4th January	500 kilos at £2.20	1,100
	100 kilos at £2.00	1,300
Value of remaining stock	(900 kilos)	1,800

Average price £

Receipts:

1st January	1,000 kilos at £2.00 per kilo	2,000
2nd January	1,000 kilos at £2.20 per kilo	2,200
Total stock	2,000 kilos	4,200

Issues of materials:

3rd January	500 kilos at £2.10	1,050
Value of remaining stock	(1,500 kilos)	3,150

Issues of materials:

4th January	600 kilos at £2.10	1,260
Value of remaining stock	(900 kilos)	1,890

2.8 Costing for labour

Labour costing is closely related to the method of remuneration operated by the organisation. Methods include:

❏ *time-based schemes,* where workers are paid a basic rate per time period;

❏ *performance-based (incentive) schemes,* where workers are paid on the basis of output;

❏ *straight piecework schemes*, where workers are paid an agreed amount for each unit produced or piecework time is paid for each unit produced;

❏ *premium bonus schemes*, where a time allowance is given for each job and a bonus is paid for any time saved.

The documents used in labour costing depend largely on the method of payment used. The main ones used are:

❏ *clock cards*, which record attendance time;

❏ daily or weekly *time sheets*, countersigned by a supervisor, which record how workers have spent their time;

❏ *job cards*, which refer to a batch or single job and record how long each Activity takes to pass through the production process;

❏ *piecework tickets*, which refer to each stage of manufacture.

Activity

Describe two work situations where you consider it would be preferable to adopt the time-based method of remuneration rather than an performance-based scheme.

It is impossible to use an performance-based scheme if the output cannot be measured reliably. It is preferable to adopt the time-based method of remuneration where quality is important, even if the output can be measured. This avoids the obvious danger of the quality of output suffering if workers have a monetary incentive to achieve high outputs.

2.9 Summary

In this chapter you have looked at what is meant by the term cost and you should now understand what cost units and cost centres are. You have examined a number of different ways in which costs can be classified and how they can be used to provide information which is useful to managers.

Further reading

Bendrey, Mike, Hussey, Roger, West, Colston, *Accounting and Finance for Business Students*, DP Publications, 3rd Edition, 1994, Chapter 27.

Drury, Colin, *Cost and Management Accounting*, Chapman & Hall, 1992, Chapter 2.

Dyson, J. R., *Accounting for Non-Accounting Students*, Pitman, 1991, Chapters 10 and 11.

Hussey, Roger, *Cost and Management Accounting*, Macmillan Professional Masters, 1989, Chapter 2.

Exercises

Progress questions

These questions have been designed to help you remember the key points in this chapter. The answers to these questions are given on page 94 at the back of this book.

Complete the following sentences:

1. A cost unit can be defined as ....

2. Direct costs can be identified with ....

3. In the short term, fixed costs tend to ....

4. The average cost per unit can be misleading if ....

5. Labour costing is closely related to ....

Select the correct response to the following statements:

6. Total variable costs stay the same when activity increases.

    True ☐ False ☐

7. Fixed costs per unit decrease as activity increases.

    True ☐ False ☐

8. LIFO is the best method for pricing material issues.

    True ☐ False ☐

9. Supervisors' salaries are an indirect cost.

    True ☐ False ☐

10. Direct materials plus direct wages plus direct expenses equals prime cost.

    True ☐ False ☐

Review questions

These questions have been designed to help you check your comprehension of the key points in this chapter. You may wish to look further than the text in this chapter in order to answer them fully. You will find your library useful as a source of wider reading. You can check your answers by referring to the appropriate section.

11. Describe the main classifications of cost. (Section 2.4)

12. What are the main elements of cost? (Section 2.5)

13. Describe the procedures for costing materials. (Section 2.6)

14. Outline the main methods of remuneration which may be used in an organisation. (Section 2.8)

Multiple choice questions

The answers to these questions will be given in the Lecturer's Supplement.

15. An example of a direct cost is:
    a) sub-contract work
    b) factory foreman's wages
    c) electricity to power a grinding machine
    d) none of these

16. An example of a production overhead is:
    a) sub-contract work
    b) piecework
    c) depreciation of managing director's Jaguar
    d) factory cleaning costs

17. If a cost is described as fixed, when activity doubles the cost per unit:
    a) remains constant
    b) doubles
    c) halves
    d) none of these

18. If a cost is described as variable, when activity doubles the cost per unit:
    a) remains constant
    b) doubles
    c) halves
    d) none of these

19. A goods received note is used to:
    a) issue materials from store
    b) check the goods sent by the supplier
    c) price the issue of material used in production
    d) return unwanted materials to the supplier

Practice questions

A marking guide to these questions will be given in the Lecturer's Supplement.

20. Explain the difference between LIFO and FIFO.

21. Explain why it is important to classify costs.

22. Describe the main documents used in costing for materials.

Questions for advanced students

A marking guide to these questions will be given in the Lecturer's Supplement.

23. Describe three methods of pricing material issues. Illustrate your answer with a worked example.

24. What problems might arise in recording direct labour costs and how would you attempt to remedy them?

Assignment: Julie's Jardinières

A marking guide to this assignment will be given in the Lecturer's Supplement.

Julie's Jardinières manufactures a range of ornamental plant pots. The firm plans to produce 2,000 units over the next month. Each variety takes about the same amount of materials and time to produce. Costs for the month are as follows:

	£
Rent:	
factory	500
office	100
Rates:	
factory	300
office	100
Sand	1,000
Power	700
Light and heat:	
factory	2,000
office	1,300
Wages:	
operators	10,000
maintenance	1,500
canteen	2,500
Cement	5,000
Depreciation:	
office equipment	500
moulds	2,200
fixtures and fittings	800
Salesmen's salary and commission	2,200
Delivery expenses	500
Office salaries	1,800
Cement mixer repairs	900
Salesmen's car expenses	1,100
Finishing paint	200
Packing	800

Julie, the owner of the business, finds the list of information somewhat confusing and asks if you can draw it up in a more structured format, identifying important figures and explaining what they mean.

Required

Prepare a report for Julie's Jardinières which provides the following financial information for the costs in total and per pot, and explain any terms used.

i)   prime cost

ii) production cost

iii) total cost

iv) administration overheads

v)   selling overheads

vi) distribution overheads

3 Total costing

3.1 Introduction

This chapter explains how overheads are charged to cost centres and cost units so that a business can calculate the total cost of an individual cost unit.

On completing this chapter you should be able to:

- ❏ describe the various stages in costing overheads;
- ❏ complete an overhead analysis;
- ❏ discuss the problems associated with costing overheads;
- ❏ calculate the total cost of a product or service.

3.2 Calculating total costs

In Chapter 2 we looked at a number of ways in which costs can be classified. One way is to divide them into *direct costs* and *indirect costs*.

> **Activity**
>
> Country Pine is a small business in the Forest of Dean which manufactures pine tables. It has one production department and makes only one style of table. Materials for the table cost £25. Labour costs are £18. The company manufactures 1,000 tables per annum and the total production overhead cost is £36,000. What is the total production cost of each table?

You should have had no problem in deciding that the total direct cost is £43, which is made up of £25 for materials and £18 for labour. However, the total cost must include a fair share of the production overheads, but what is a fair share? As the organisation is only making tables and they are all the same, a fair method would be to divide the total overhead cost by the total number of units produced:

$$\frac{£36,000}{1,000} = £36$$

The following statement draws these calculations together to show the total production cost of one table.

Total production cost of one table

	£
Direct costs:	
Materials	25
Labour	18
Production overheads	36
Total production cost	79

Unfortunately, this method cannot be used very often because businesses are rarely organised as simply as this. There are often a number of different departments with a range of activities; some departments may not be production departments but service departments which provide maintenance facilities, storage facilities, administrative support, selling and distribution or canteen facilities. In addition, there may be a range of goods, rather than a single product, each spending different lengths of time in the production department and making unequal demands on resources. In such a situation, the above method is not a fair way of sharing overheads over production.

3.3 Allocating and apportioning production overheads

To overcome this difficulty we can use a technique called *absorption costing*. This allows us to charge overheads to cost units by means of rates calculated separately for different cost centres. The technique seeks to provide answers to two problems:

i) how to share the total overheads of the organisation over the various production departments;

ii) how to share the overheads for a particular production department over the various products passing through it.

Activity

In the previous example of Country Pine Ltd, was the method used a solution to problem i) or problem ii) above?

The method used was a solution to problem ii) because we were looking at a small organisation which had only one production department. By dividing the total overhead by the number of tables, we shared the overheads over the products passing through it.

Usually we have to solve the first problem before we can tackle the second. You will remember from Chapter 2 that overheads can be classified by *nature,* such as rent, wages and depreciation. When overheads are classified in this way, they fall into two main groups. The first group are those which can be wholly identified with one particular *cost centre*; for example, all the depreciation charge on machinery may be due to only one particular production department. This process of charging to one particular cost centre is called *cost allocation*.

The second group of overheads are those which cannot be identified with a single cost centre, but must be shared or *apportioned* over all the cost centres benefiting from them. This process is known as *cost apportionment;* for example, factory rent might be apportioned over the cost centres on the basis of the space that they occupy.

To charge overheads to cost centres by allocation and apportionment an *overhead analysis* is prepared. This shows the overheads by their nature and the total cost of each one. The various costs centres are shown at the top of the analysis.

Activity

Just Jackets Ltd makes leather jackets. It has a cutting department where the jackets are cut out by sophisticated machines and a stitching department where they are sewed and finished by machinists. Some of the overheads have been allocated from information available within the business; others must be apportioned. The following information should help you decide what would be a fair way of sharing them over the two cost centres.

	Cutting department	Stitching department
Production area	250 sq metres	150 sq metres
Number of employees	5	15
Value of machinery	£100,000	£20,0000
Value of stock	£40,000	£80,0000

Complete the following overhead analysis. First decide and enter the basis of apportionment and then calculate the portion of the total overhead to be borne by each cost centre. Of the overhead costs, indirect materials and labour have been allocated and entered for you. The rent has also been apportioned to show you the method.

Rent is best apportioned on the basis of the area occupied. The total area is 250 + 150 = 400 square metres and the rent is £12,000. Therefore the rent can be apportioned as follows:

Cutting department: $\dfrac{250}{400} \times £12,000 = £7,500$

Stitching department: $\dfrac{150}{400} \times £12,000 = £4,500$

Overhead analysis

Overhead	Total cost £	Basis of apportionment	Cutting dept. £	Stitching dept. £
Indirect materials	40,000	Allocated	17,500	22,500
Indirect labour	17,100	Allocated	4,200	12,900
Rent	12,000	Area	7,500	4,500
Electricity	4,000			
Depreciation on machinery	9,000			
Supervisors' salaries	22,000			
Stock insurance	900			
Total	105,000			

After deciding a fair way of apportioning the overheads, the calculations should not have presented any great problems. Check your completed overhead analysis against the following:

Overhead analysis

Overhead	Total cost £	Basis of apportionment	Cutting dept. £	Stitching dept. £
Indirect materials	40,000	Allocated	17,500	22,500
Indirect labour	17,100	Allocated	4,200	12,900
Rent	12,000	Area	7,500	4,500
Electricity	4,000	Area	2,500	1,500
Depreciation on machinery	9,000	Value of machinery	7,500	1,500
Supervisors' salaries	22,000	Number of employees	5,500	16,500
Stock insurance	900	Value of stock	300	600
Total	105,000		45,000	60,000

If your analysis differs from the above, it may be because you decided on different bases of apportionment, so we will look at the reasons for making particular choices. Both rent and electricity would seem to be best shared on the basis of the area occupied by that cost centre. Depreciation is clearly related to the value of the machinery used in each cost centre. The supervisors' salaries are more problematical. In the absence of any other information, we have assumed that they are related to the number of employees. You might argue that they could be related to floor space and in some circumstances you would be right. Finally, the stock insurance is clearly based on the value of the stock and therefore it has been allocated on that basis.

Agreeing on a fair way to apportion overheads is a major difficulty in many organisations and you may still disagree with the reasons given above. However, the guiding principle is to be consistent and to choose a method which appears to be fair from the information provided. In section 3.6 we will look at the problem of service cost centres, but at this stage we will concentrate on our two production departments.

We now know that the total overhead cost for the cutting department is £45,000 and £60,000 for the finishing department. Next we must decide how we are going to share these overheads between all the jackets passing through the two departments.

3.4 Overhead cost absorption

At the beginning of this chapter we stated that if all the products were the same, we could simply divide the total overhead costs by the number of cost units. The method of charging overheads to cost units is known as *overhead recovery* or *overhead absorption* rate. If it is calculated on the number of units, as in the Country Pine example, we are using the *cost unit overhead absorption rate*. The most appropriate overhead absorption rate depends on the resources used and the way we measure them.

There are a number of methods used to charge overheads to the cost unit. To use the cost unit itself as the basis for the calculation is the simplest. It is done by dividing the production overheads for each production department by the number of cost units passing through them. This gives an overhead absorption rate for each department.

Activity

Just Jackets Ltd manufactures two styles of jacket: classic and designer. In one year, 4,000 classic jackets are made and 1,000 designer jackets. What is the total overhead cost for each jacket if you use the cost unit overhead absorption rate?

The calculation of the total overhead cost per jacket needs some care. You should have remembered that each jacket must pass through the cutting department and the stitching department. Therefore, the overhead absorption rate must be calculated separately for each department and then added together. Your answer should have been calculated as follows:

Overhead absorption rate	*Cutting department*	*Stitching department*
Cost units	$\dfrac{£45,000}{5,000} = £9$ per cost unit	$\dfrac{£60,000}{5,000} = £12$ per cost unit

Therefore, the total overhead cost is £9 + £12 = £21 per cost unit.

Although using cost units is the easiest method, it would be unfair to charge the same overhead to the different styles of jackets if the more expensive jackets use up more of the resources. It is fairer to make sure that the product which uses up more of the resources bears more of the overhead.

Activity

If you took your car to the garage to have the brakes adjusted and you were charged the same overhead charge as someone who has had a full service, you would be very upset. It would not help if the garage owner told you that he had worked out his overhead charge by dividing his total overheads by the number of cars repaired. What basis would you suggest the garage uses for charging overheads on the work done?

You may have suggested that overheads are charged on a time basis. Garages usually charge an hourly rate for repairs, as do many other businesses, such as plumbers and electricians. The hourly rate can be calculated on the basis of the time an employee spends working on the product, the direct labour hour rate, or on how long the product is on a machine, the machine hour rate.

Activity

Returning to our example of Just Jackets Ltd, calculate an hourly overhead rate for each department based either on direct labour hours or machine hours. The following table gives details of how many *direct labour hours* and *machine hours* are required in each department to make the 5,000 jackets.

Overhead absorption rate	*Cutting department*	*Stitching department*
Direct labour hours	10,000	30,000
Machine hours	40,000	5,000

You may have found this difficult. You should have divided the overheads for each department first by the total number of direct labour hours and then by the total number of machine hours to give the absorption rates.

Overhead absorption rate	Cutting department	Stitching department
Direct labour hours	$\dfrac{£45,000}{10,000} = £4.50$	$\dfrac{£60,000}{30,000} = £2.00$
Machine hours	$\dfrac{£45,000}{40,000} = £1.13$	$\dfrac{£60,000}{5,000} = £12.00$

We have now calculated three different overhead absorption rates for each department. The *overhead absorption rate* gives us a method of charging the total overheads of the department to all the cost units passing through it. The *cost unit overhead absorption rate* was calculated by dividing the overheads for the department by the total number of cost units. The *direct labour hour overhead absorption rate* was calculated by dividing the overheads for the department by the total number of direct labour hours. Finally, the *machine hour overhead absorption rate* was calculated by dividing the overheads for the department by the total number of machine hours. There are other types of overhead absorption rates which are used, often based on a percentage calculation, but we will concentrate on these three as they are the most important.

The following table summarises the information we have so far:

	Cutting department	Stitching department
Total overheads	£45,000	£60,000
Number of cost units	5,000	5,000
Direct labour hours	10,000	30,000
Machine hours	40,000	5,000
Overhead absorption rates:		
Cost unit	£9.00	£12.00
Direct labour hour	£4.50	£2.00
Machine hour	£1.13	£12.00

For illustrative purposes we have calculated three types of overhead rate, but only one will be used in each department. Now we need to select the fairest rate for each department for charging the overhead to each jacket.

Activity

Which of the three overhead absorption rates do you think is the most appropriate for use in each of the departments? (The same rate need not be used in both departments.)

As already pointed out, it would be unfair to use the cost unit absorption rate because the two types of jacket use unequal amounts of resources. With the other two rates you should have considered the main resources being provided in each department by the expenditure on overheads. You will see that in the cutting department the overheads have been incurred mainly in the supply of machine hours. Therefore, this is the most appropriate basis for calculating the overhead absorption rate. In the finishing department the work is mainly manual and therefore the direct labour hour rate would be the most appropriate overhead absorption rate.

3.5 Calculating the total unit cost

We have now reached the final and most important stage of our calculations, which is to find out the total cost of making each classic jacket and each designer jacket.

Although we have spent some time learning how the overheads are calculated, we must not forget to charge for the direct materials and direct labour.

Activity

Calculate the total production cost of each style of jacket from the following information using the pro forma below.

	Classic jacket	Designer jacket
Direct materials	£50	£80
Direct labour	£20	£40
Cutting department machine hours	7	12
Stitching department direct labour hours	5	10

Total cost of one jacket

	Classic jacket	Designer jacket
	£	£
Direct materials		
Direct labour		
Overheads:		
Cutting department		
(£1.13 per machine hour)		
Stitching department		
(£2.00 per direct labour hour)		
Total production cost		

Your completed statement should look like this:

Total cost of one jacket

	Classic jacket	Designer jacket
	£	£
Direct materials	50.00	80.00
Direct labour	20.00	40.00
Overheads:		
Cutting department		
(£1.13 per machine hour)	7.91	13.56
Stitching department		
(£2.00 per direct labour hour)	10.00	20.00
Total production cost	87.91	153.56

3.6 Service cost centres

So far, we have only considered production cost centres. However, most businesses also have *service cost centres*. Examples include departments which are associated with the production areas, such as maintenance, stores and canteen, and others which are not, such as administration, sales and distribution.

The first stage is to calculate the total production cost as before, but this time we will include the service cost centres associated with the production area. We will deal with other overheads later. The same procedure is used; the different types of production overheads are allocated and apportioned, and subtotalled. Then the subtotal of the service cost centres is apportioned to the production cost centres on a fair basis.

Activity

Country Pine Ltd, the business we looked at earlier, has expanded and now makes quality bookcases of different sizes. The following information is available.

	Joinery department	Finishing department	Maintenance department
Area	200 sq metres	200 sq metres	100 sq metres
Number of employees	12	16	4
Value of machinery	£250,000	£100,000	£50,000

Now complete the following overhead analysis by showing the basis of apportionment and the total overhead to be borne by each of the three production cost centres. The allocated overhead costs have been entered for you. Once you have arrived at a subtotal for all three cost centres, you must apportion the total for the maintenance department, which is a service department, over the two production departments on whatever basis you consider appropriate.

Overhead analysis

Overhead	Total cost	Basis of apportion- ment	Joinery department	Finishing department	Maintenance department
	£		£	£	£
Indirect materials	10,000	Allocated	6,000	3,000	1,000
Indirect labour	31,500	Allocated	4,000	8,000	19,500
Rent	20,000				
Electricity	5,000				
Depreciation on machinery	40,000				
Supervisors' salaries	36,000				
Subtotal	142,500				
Apportioned service cost centre	-				
Total	142,500				

Check your answer against the following:

Overhead analysis

Overhead	Total cost	Basis of apportion- ment	Joinery department	Finishing department	Maintenance department
	£		£	£	£
Indirect materials	10,000	Allocated	6,000	3,000	1,000
Indirect labour	31,500	Allocated	4,000	8,000	19,500
Rent	20,000	Area	8,000	8,000	4,000
Electricity	5,000	Area	2,000	2,000	1,000
Depreciation on machinery	40,000	Value of Machinery	25,000	10,000	5,000
Supervisors' salaries	36,000	Number of employees	13,500	18,000	4,500
Subtotal	142,500		58,500	49,000	45,000
Apportioned service cost centre	-	Value of machinery	25,000	10,000	(35,000)
Total	142,500		83,500	59,000	-

The subtotal of the maintenance department has been apportioned to the two production departments on the basis of the value of the machinery in the production department. The value of the machinery in the maintenance department itself is excluded from the calculations.

Activity

Continuing the above example, the overhead absorption rate in the joinery department is based on 10,000 machine hours and in the finishing department on 30,000 direct labour hours. Calculate the two overhead absorption rates in the joinery and finishing departments.

The answer is calculated by dividing the total cost centre overhead for the period by the number of units of the basis of absorption; in this case, machine hours in the joinery department and direct labour hours in the finishing department. The correct answer is:

Joinery department: $\dfrac{£83,500}{10,000} = £8.35$ per machine hour

Finishing department: $\dfrac{£59,000}{30,000} = £1.97$ per direct labour hour

Activity

A customer puts in an order for a bookcase for which the direct costs are as follows:

Direct materials £80.00
Direct labour £50.00

It is estimated that the bookcase will require 8 machine hours in the joinery department and 10 labour hours in the finishing department. Calculate the total production cost.

Your answer should look like this:

	£
Direct materials	80.00
Direct labour	50.00
Overheads:	
Joinery (8 hours at £8.35)	66.80
Finishing (10 hours at £1.97)	19.70
Total production cost	216.50

What we have just calculated is the total production cost, but in order to find out the total cost of the bookcase, we need to add the administration, selling and distribution overheads. This can be done by adding a percentage figure using the following formula:

$$\frac{\text{Total administration and selling overheads}}{\text{Total production costs}} \times 100$$

First you should have calculated the percentage to be added to the total production cost:

$$\frac{£46,000}{£230,000} \times 100 = 20\%$$

Next you need to do the calculation:

	£
Total production cost	216.50
Add 20%	43.30
Total cost	259.80

3.7 Predetermined overhead absorption rates

So far we have implied that the absorption rates are based on actual costs, but in practice these costs are predetermined. Before the start of a financial period, which may be as short as a month or as long as a year for this purpose, decisions will be made on the likely level of activity and the probable costs which will be incurred during the period. In Chapter 6 we will be looking at *budgetary control,* which is the process of establishing financial plans, in detail.

Once the likely level of activity has been decided, the amount of machine hours, labour hours and overheads which are likely to incurred can be determined. This allows a *predetermined overhead absorption rate* to be calculated at the beginning of a period and applied throughout. The actual costs are not used because the collection, analysis and absorption of overheads to products or jobs takes a considerable time, and the actual figures may not be available until after the end of the financial period. Naturally it would be impossible to wait until then to invoice customers, submit estimates, make decisions on production methods or carry out any other management task.

The main problems are that the actual overheads are very likely to differ from those budgeted; the actual base of absorption may differ from the budget; or a combination of these two factors. This can have serious consequences. If an organisation has been invoicing customers on a predetermined overhead rate which is wrong, it could have significant impact on profits. Where the overheads charged to production are higher than the actual overheads for the period, the variance is known as *over absorption*. In other words, too much overhead has been charged to production. Where the overheads charged to production are lower than the actual overheads, the variance is known as *under absorption*.

Although we have used the manufacture of tables and jackets in this chapter as examples, the same principles of allocating, apportioning and absorbing overheads apply in all organisations where management wants to know the total cost of a product, service or department.

3.8 Summary

In this chapter we have looked at the methods used to calculate the total cost of a product or service. You have drawn up an overhead analysis and learnt how overheads are either allocated or apportioned to cost centres. You have examined the various methods for charging the overheads of a cost centre to the cost units passing through it and calculated the total cost of a product. In addition, you have looked at the practical problems which may arise and how they can be resolved.

Further reading

Drury, Colin, *Costing: An Introduction*, Chapman & Hall, 1990, Chapter 8.

Dyson, J. R., *Accounting for Non-Accounting Students*, Pitman, 1991, Chapters 10 and 13.

Glautier, M. W. E., Underdown, B., *Accounting Theory and Practice*, Pitman, 1991, Chapter 31.

Izhar, Riad, *Accounting, Costing and Management*, Oxford University Press, 1990, Chapter 16.

Exercises

Progress questions

These questions have been designed to help you remember the key points in this chapter. The answers to these questions are given on page 94 at the back of this book.

Complete the following sentences:

1. Cost apportionment is ....

2. An overhead analysis allows ....

3. The overhead absorption rate is the method for ....

4. The overheads for service cost centres must be ....

5. The direct labour hour absorption rate is calculated by ....

Select the correct response to the following statements:

6. Cost allocation is a technique for charging overheads to cost units.

True ☐ False ☐

7. Cost apportionment is the process of sharing overhead costs between two or more cost centres in proportion to the benefit they receive.

True ☐ False ☐

8. Absorption costing can be used where the cost centre caused the overhead to be incurred and the exact amount is known.

True ☐ False ☐

9. It is always best to use the direct labour hour absorption rate.

True ☐ False ☐

10. The overheads of service cost centres are not part of the total cost of a unit.

True ☐ False ☐

Review questions

These questions have been designed to help you check your comprehension of the key points in this chapter. You may wish to look further than the text in this chapter in order to answer them fully. You will find your library useful as a source of wider reading. You can check your answers by referring to the appropriate section.

11. Draw up a list of the main stages in finding out the total cost of a product. (Sections 3.3 and 3.4)

12. What are the two main problems in charging overheads to cost units? (Section 3.3)

13. Describe three overhead cost absorption rates. (Section 3.4)

14. What are predetermined overhead absorption rates? (Section 3.7)

Multiple choice questions

The answers to these questions will be given in the Lecturer's Supplement.

15. Costs must be allocated to a cost centre or cost unit if they are:
    a) indirect costs
    b) direct costs
    c) production overheads
    d) other overheads

16. The reasons for charging costs to cost centres are:
    a) to determine the costs of operating a cost centre
    b) to enable overheads to be charged to products
    c) neither of these
    d) both of these

17. A cost centre may be:
    a) a complete product
    b) a sub-assembly
    c) a unit of production
    d) none of these

18. A cost unit may be:
    a) a department
    b) a factory
    c) neither of these
    d) both of these

19. In calculating total unit cost, service cost centres in the factory are best:
    a) ignored completely
    b) added to selling and distribution overheads
    c) apportioned to production cost centres
    d) charged to cost units

Practice questions

A marking guide to these questions will be given in the Lecturer's Supplement.

20. In what circumstances would you recommend the use of the machine hour overhead absorption rate?

21. Describe the treatment of administration, selling and distribution overheads in calculating total unit cost.

22. Distinguish between overhead allocation and overhead apportionment.

Questions for advanced students

A marking guide to these questions will be given in the Lecturer's Supplement.

23. What are the advantages and disadvantages of using a 'factory wide' overhead absorption rate?

24. Describe the most appropriate way of dealing with under or over absorption of overheads.

Assignment: West Wales Windsurfers Ltd

A marking guide to this assignment will be given in the Lecturer's Supplement.

West Wales Windsurfers Ltd make two models of windsurfer. The company has two production departments: a shaping department and a finishing department. It also has a canteen which serves all the employees. The budgeted sales and costs for the next year are as follows:

	Fun wave	Hot racer
Selling price per unit	£600	£700
Sales/production volume	2,000 units	2,500 units
Material costs per unit	£80	£50
Direct labour:		
Shaping dept (£3 per hour)	50 hours per unit	60 hours per unit
Finishing dept (£2 per hour)	40 hours per unit	40 hours per unit
Machine hours:		
Shaping dept	30 hours per unit	80 hours per unit
Finishing department	10 hours per unit	

	Shaping department	Finishing department	Canteen	Total
	£	£	£	£
Production overheads:				
Variable	260,000	90,000	-	350,000
Fixed	420,000	300,000	160,000	880,000
Total	680,000	390,000	160,000	1,230,000
Number of employees	150	90	10	
Floor area (sq metres)	40,000	10,000	10,000	

Required

i) Advise the company on the method of overhead absorption which should be used for each department. Give reasons for your choice.

ii) Calculate an appropriate overhead absorption rate for each production department.

iii) Calculate the total budgeted cost per unit of each model of windsurfer.

4 Marginal costing

4.1 Introduction

This chapter investigates the impact of changes in the volume of activity undertaken by a business on costs and profits.

On completing this chapter you should be able to:

- ❏ differentiate between fixed and variable costs;
- ❏ draw up a marginal cost statement;
- ❏ explain the importance of calculating the contribution;
- ❏ calculate the break-even point of an activity;
- ❏ describe the effect of limiting factors.

4.2 Cost behaviour

In Chapter 2 that we defined *direct costs* as those costs which can be identified with a specific product or saleable service, and *indirect* costs as those which cannot. We defined *fixed* costs as those costs which in total tend to remain the same regardless of changes in the level of activity, and *variable* costs as those which in total tend to change in direct proportion to changes in the level of activity. From this we can deduce that *direct* costs will always be *variable* costs.

The words 'tend to change' are used in the definition because there is not always a direct relationship and some costs are *semi-variable*. This means that they contain both a fixed and a variable element. A marginal cost is regarded by accountants as the average variable cost and is assumed to be constant in the short-term.

Activity

Identify which of the costs in the following list are normally classified as fixed and which are normally classified as variable in a manufacturing organisation.

	Fixed cost	Variable cost
Accountants' salaries		
Advertising		
Depreciation		
Direct labour		
Direct materials		
Machine operators' wages		
Rates		
Rent		
Salesmen's commission		
Warehouse wages		

Even if you do not have any experience of working in a manufacturing environment you should have been able to identify these from the definitions of fixed and variable costs. Accountants' salaries, advertising, depreciation, rates, rent and warehouse wages are all examples of fixed costs. Direct labour, direct materials, machine operators' wages and salesmen's commission are usually considered as variable costs because they change when the level of activity changes.

Activity

In Sam Reeve's taxi business, which we used as an example in Chapter 2, the average mileage by a taxi in one quarter is 15,000 miles and the costs, analysed by nature, are as follows:

Expense	Total for quarter
	£
Driver's salary	2,670
Petrol and oil	1,050
Annual service	450
Taxation and insurance	1,110
Depreciation	870
Total	6,150

Sam has been invited to submit a quotation for a special job which will involve an additional 500 miles per quarter. This mileage can be done in the driver's current time allowance, so no additional salary will be incurred. Sam needs to know the costs of the additional 500 miles per quarter, so that he can quote for the job.

Explain how the following figures have been calculated. Is any of them the correct figure of cost for the additional 500 miles?

i) £205

ii) £116

iii) £35

If we look at how the figures are calculated, we will see that the first answer, £205, is the result of multiplying the mileage of 500 miles by the total cost per mile of 41p. The total cost per mile is calculated by dividing the total cost for the quarter by the average mileage for the quarter of 15,000 miles. However, we know that no additional wages for the driver will be incurred, so it would be incorrect to take £205 as the cost of the additional 500 miles. The driver's wages, in this example, can be considered as a *fixed cost*. In our example, activity is measured in miles.

The second answer, £116, has been calculated by multiplying the 500 miles by 23.2p; that is, the total cost per mile less the driver's element. But this is not the correct answer to the question, because if you look at the list of costs you will see that the driver's salary is not the only fixed cost. Certain other costs will not increase because of the additional 500 miles per quarter.

Activity

What other costs would you consider to be mainly fixed in Sam's list of expenses?

Taking them in the order in which they are listed, the costs for petrol and oil will obviously rise with the increased mileage, so they are not fixed. With regard to servicing and repairs, some routine servicing will be carried out regardless of the mileage and this is therefore a fixed cost. However, other servicing and repair costs depend on the mileage. Clearly, tax and insurance are fixed costs and, like the driver's salary, should be excluded from our calculations of the cost for the additional 500 miles. Depreciation, to some extent, is influenced by the amount of mileage, but in a taxi business, depreciation depends mainly on the passage of time.

The above identification of fixed costs should help you with the third answer suggested, £35. This has been calculated by multiplying the 500 miles by 7p, the cost of petrol and oil per mile. In view of the information we have available, this is the best answer. If we are to be more precise, we will need more details of the service and repair costs so that we can identify which are fixed.

Activity

Circle the correct answer in the following statements:

i) If activity increases the total fixed cost will increase/decrease/stay the same.

ii) If activity increases the fixed cost per unit will increase/decrease/stay the same.

iii) If activity decreases the total fixed cost will increase/decrease/stay the same.

iv) If activity decreases the fixed cost per unit will increase/decrease/stay the same.

You should have had little difficulty in deciding the answers to i) and iii). These are drawn straight from the definition and in both cases the total fixed costs stay the same regardless of changes in the level of activity. You may have found the answers to ii) and iv) a little more difficult and some simple figures may help. We will take as our example a factory where the rent is £8,000 per annum, a fixed cost. The output of the factory each year is 1,000 units. The cost for rent per unit is therefore £8. If the factory makes 1,500 units one year, what is the rent per unit? The total rent cost will stay the same at £8,000 so the cost per unit for rent will decrease to £5.33. Therefore, the answer to ii) is that if activity increases the fixed cost per unit will decrease. The reasoning is similar with statement iv): if activity decreases the fixed cost per unit will increase.

Activity

Circle the correct answer in the following statements:

i) If activity increases, the total variable cost will increase/decrease/stay the same.

ii) If activity increases, the variable cost per unit will increase/decrease/stay the same.

iii) If activity decreases, the total variable cost will increase/decrease/stay the same.

iv) If activity decreases, the variable cost per unit will increase/decrease/stay the same

You should have found this activity fairly straightforward after the earlier example. The answer to statements ii) and iv) is that if activity increases or decreases the variable cost per unit will stay the same. The answer to statement i) is that when activity increases the total variable cost will increase. Similarly with statement iii), when activity decreases, the total variable cost decreases.

4.3 Calculating contribution

In Chapter 3 we examined absorption costing, which is a method of charging *all costs* to the product or service. *Marginal costing* is a technique whereby only the *variable or marginal* costs of production are charged to the cost units. Marginal costing is sometimes called direct costing and in some text books it is described under the heading of cost-volume-profit analysis. The advantage of marginal costing over absorption costing is that it recognises that costs behave differently as activity changes.

As we saw in the previous section, *total fixed costs* tend to remain the same despite changes in levels of production or sales activity. *Total variable costs* tend to increase or decrease in line with production or sales activity. *Semi-variable costs* contain both fixed and variable cost elements and must be analysed so that the fixed cost elements can be added to other fixed costs and the variable cost elements to the other variable costs. Because some costs change and others stay the same when activity changes, so the total cost for all production and the total cost per unit changes, but not directly. We therefore need a technique which will provide useful information if we are interested in an organisation where activity levels fluctuate. Marginal costing is such a technique.

Under marginal costing, only the variable costs are charged to the units. The difference between the selling price and the variable cost is not a profit, since no allowance has been made for fixed costs. The difference between the selling price and the variable costs per unit is the *contribution* (to fixed costs) and can be calculated for one unit or for any chosen level of sales. As soon as the total fixed costs have been covered by the contribution, the organisation starts making a profit.

Activity

Mementoes Ltd manufactures ceramic models of historic buildings for the tourist trade. The materials for each model cost 60p and the labour costs are 30p per unit. The presentation boxes cost 15p per unit. The selling price is £2.30 each. The total fixed costs or overheads for the business are £850 per week. The normal weekly output is 1,000 units. Complete the following marginal cost statement, calculating the contribution per 1,000 units and per single unit.

Mementoes Ltd
Marginal cost statement for one week

	1,000 units		1 unit	
	£	£	£	£
Sales		2,300		2.30
Variable costs:				
Materials				
Labour				
Packaging				
Contribution				
Less Total fixed costs				
Net profit/(loss)				

You should not have had too much difficulty with this if you remembered that contribution is the difference between the selling price and the unit variable costs. Your completed marginal cost statement should look like this:

Mementoes Ltd
Marginal cost statement for one week

	1,000 units		1 unit	
	£	£	£	£
Sales		2,300		2.30
Variable costs:				
Materials	600		0.60	
Labour	300		0.30	
Packaging	150	1,050	0.15	1.05
Contribution		1,250		1.25
Less Total fixed costs		850		
Net profit/(loss)		400		

Marginal costing is useful for a number of short-term decisions such as:

❏ setting the selling price of products, particularly in times of trade depression and when introducing new products;

❏ evaluating the proposed closure or temporary cessation of part of the business;

❏ deciding the value of accepting a special contract or order;

❏ comparing the cost implications of different methods of manufacture.

We shall now look at some examples.

Activity

What is the lowest selling price Mementoes Ltd could set for its models?

If you look back at the marginal cost statement you will see that the answer is £1.05; any lower than that would mean that the company does not recoup all the variable costs it incurs in making one unit. Even at £1.05 the company is not obtaining a contribution towards its fixed costs.

Activity

Iceblock Ltd makes three types of iced lolly and shares its fixed overheads equally over the three types. A summary of the financial statement for last month is shown below.

	Fruit Ice	Choc Ice	Kool Ice
Total number produced	11,200	9,000	6,000
	£	£	£
Total sales	5,500	4,500	2,400
Variable costs	2,400	1,800	1,300
Contribution	3,100	2,700	1,100
Fixed costs	2,000	2,000	2,000
Net profit/(loss)	1,100	700	(900)

The sales director has suggested that as sales of all ice lollies are expected to decrease by 10% next month, production of Kool Ice should be stopped until demand picks up. Redraft the above statement, first showing what will happen if there is a 10% decrease in demand, and second, if production of Kool Ice is halted.

Check your answer against the following figures:

	Fruit Ice	Choc Ice	Kool Ice	Total
Total number produced	10,080	8,100	5,400	
	£	£	£	£
Total sales	4,950	4,050	2,160	11,160
Variable costs	2,160	1,620	1,170	4,950
Contribution	2,790	2,430	990	6,210
Fixed costs	2,000	2,000	2,000	6,000
Net profit/(loss)	790	430	(1,010)	210

The above statement shows the impact of the 10% decrease on profit as well as the fact that Kool Ice is making a contribution to fixed costs. If production of Kool Ice is stopped, than the net profit would turn into a net loss as follows:

	£
Contribution:	
Fruit Ice	2,790
Choc Ice	2,430
	5,220
Less Fixed costs	6,000
Net loss	(780)

The loss which results is because we assume that the £6,000 of fixed costs will stay the same, at least in the short term, regardless of changes in activity or the cessation of one of the product lines. The general rule is that, if a product or service makes a contribution towards fixed costs, it is financially worthwhile continuing to provide it. There may be other business reasons for dropping it or it may be financially preferable to direct the activities of the organisation in another direction. But in the above example it is financially advisable to continue production of Kool Ice.

Activity

A large hotel has approached Iceblock Ltd and offers to place an order for 600 Kool Ices per month if the price is reduced from 40p to 30p per lolly. The order would restore demand, but should the company accept it in view of the low price offered?

The general rule is that, if you have idle production capacity, it is worthwhile accepting a special order as long as it makes a contribution. The key figures for Kool Ice, calculated to the nearest penny, are as follows:

	Per unit		Per unit
Present selling price	40p	Suggested selling price	30p
Variable costs	22p	Variable costs	22p
Contribution	18p	Contribution	8p

As the special price will still give a contribution of 8p, it is worthwhile accepting. However, there may be other factors which must be considered, such as the reaction of other customers who may learn of this discounted price, before making a final decision.

Activity

The production manager says he can change the production method so that up to 12,000 Fruit Ices can be produced per month for an additional fixed cost of £500 per month. He estimates that this will save variable costs of 4p per Fruit Ice. Do you think this plan should be implemented?

There is no need to do a full calculation again, but look instead at the maximum possible savings in variable costs and compare them with the fixed costs. The maximum savings will be 4p x 12,000 = £480. Since this is lower than the £500 additional fixed costs incurred, the proposal is not worthwhile.

4.4 Limiting factors

A *limiting factor* is a key factor which constrains the growth of an organisation. Examples are sales or shortages of materials or labour. The limiting factor should be identified and production arranged so that the contribution per unit of limiting factor is maximised.

In the examples we have looked at so far in this chapter we have assumed that there are no factors present which would prevent the organisations from achieving the level of activity required to break even or to make the desired level of profit. However, this is rarely the case in business and there is nearly always some factor present, such as the maximum sales which can be made or the production capacity of machinery, which prevents unlimited growth. In making decisions using contribution, we have to take such factors into account. We can explain this by turning back to Mementoes Ltd.

Mementoes Ltd makes models of historic buildings but we said that there was only one model priced at £2.30 with variable costs of £1.05. Let us assume that this model is of Winchester Cathedral. One of their designers suggests that they make a model of Windsor Castle instead of Winchester Cathedral. The fixed costs of the business would stay the same but the variable costs and selling price would be as follows:

	Winchester Cathedral		Windsor Castle	
	£	£	£	£
Selling price		2.30		3.00
Variable costs:				
Materials	0.60		0.90	
Labour	0.30		0.35	
Packaging	0.15	1.05	0.20	1.45
Contribution		1.25		1.55

Activity

Based on the above information, do you recommend that the company makes models of Winchester Cathedral or Windsor Castle?

You should have had no difficulty with this because the contribution per unit Mementoes gets from Windsor Castle is £1.55 compared with £1.25 from Winchester Cathedral. The general rule is that if there are no limiting factors present, select the activity which gives the highest contribution. This is assuming that you are certain that you can sell them!

Activity

The company finds that the supply of materials is limited and therefore it can only make a limited number of models. It uses the same materials for both models, but as can be seen from the above costs, Windsor Castle uses 50% more materials. Which model do you recommend the company makes to obtain the maximum profit?

You may have found this slightly more difficult. When there is a particular limiting factor present, in this case it is materials, the general rule is to maximise the contribution per unit of limiting factor. In other words, select the model which gives the greatest contribution for the materials used. We do not know the amount of materials. If we did, we could calculate the contribution per kilo by dividing the contribution per unit by the number of kilos per unit. However, as we know the cost of materials for each model, we can calculate the contribution we get for each penny of materials as follows:

	Winchester Cathedral	Windsor Castle
	£	£
Contribution per unit	1.250	1.550
Materials per unit	0.600	0.900
Contribution per 1p of materials	0.208	0.172

In this example, if materials are limited it would be best to manufacture models of Winchester Cathedral since this has the highest contribution per unit per limiting factor. As you can see, if we only had £100 of materials, we could get a contribution of £20.80 from Winchester Cathedral, but only £17.20 from Windsor Castle.

4.5 Break-even analysis

Break-even analysis is an extension of marginal costing and is used to identify the *break-even* point of a business. The break-even point is where the business makes neither a profit nor a loss and can be determined by constructing a chart or by applying the following formula:

$$\text{Break-even point in units} = \frac{\text{Total fixed costs}}{\text{Contribution per unit}}$$

You will remember that contribution per unit is the selling price less the variable costs per unit. The above formula gives the same answer as would be arrived at by constructing a break-even chart, but with more complex figures it permits a greater degree of accuracy.

Activity

Mementoes Ltd sells each model for £2.30. Materials cost 60p, labour 30p and packing costs 15p per unit. The fixed costs were £850 per week. Calculate the break-even point using the above formula.

Substituting the figures for the formula, your calculations should have been as follows:

$$\text{Break-even point} = \frac{\pounds850}{\pounds1.25} = \text{approximately 680 models}$$

The sales value at the break-even point can be found by using the following formula:

$$\text{Sales value at break-even point} = \frac{\text{Total fixed costs} \times \text{Sales value}}{\text{Total contribution}}$$

The amounts for sales value and contribution can be at the maximum level of activity, per unit or any other level.

Activity

Calculate the sales value at the break-even point for Mementoes Ltd.

Substituting the figures for the formula, your calculations should have been as follows:

$$\text{Sales value at break-even point} = \frac{\pounds850 \times \pounds2,300}{\pounds1,250} = \pounds1,564$$

If the organisation has a specific target profit, the level of activity that will achieve it can be found by using the following formula:

$$\text{Selected level of activity in units} = \frac{\text{Fixed costs } + \text{ Target profit}}{\text{Contribution per unit}}$$

Activity

If Mementoes wanted to make a profit of £200 per week, how many models would have to be made and sold?

Using the above formula you should have had little difficulty in calculating the number and your answer should be:

$$\text{Selected level of activity} = \frac{£850 + £200}{£1.25} = 840 \text{ models}$$

The difference between the selected level of activity, in this case 840 models, and the break-even point of 680 models is known as the margin of safety. Mementoes could miss its target of 840 models by 160 models before it goes under the break-even point and starts making a loss.

All this information can be shown on a break-even graph. The procedure for constructing a break-even graph is as follows.

1. Draw a horizontal axis to measure activity.

2. Draw a vertical axis to measure costs and revenue.

3. Plot a fixed cost line which will be parallel to the horizontal axis.

4. Plot a total cost line by adding the variable costs to the fixed costs, remembering that at nil activity there will be no variable costs, but there will be the total fixed costs.

5. Plot the revenue line.

The point where the revenue line and the total cost line intercept is the break-even point.

Activity

Draw a break-even graph for Mementoes Ltd. Assume that the maximum level of activity is 900 models.

If you have drawn your graph accurately, you should have obtained the same break-even point as you calculated using the formula.

Your completed graph should look like this:

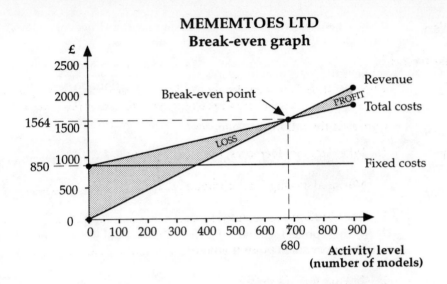

MEMEMTOES LTD
Break-even graph

Break-even analysis makes the same assumptions about the behaviour of fixed and variable costs as marginal costing. These rarely hold true over a complete range of activity and a period of time. Fixed costs may move in steps as additional facilities such as another machine, more factory space, etc., are brought into use as production increases. Variable costs may rise steeply in the early stages because production is not very efficient. They may also rise again at the peak of activity due to pressure of work causing inefficiencies.

In this section we have concentrated on calculating the break-even point. However, the same principles can be used for calculating the profit at different levels of activity. For this reason, some text books prefer to use the term *cost-volume-profit* analysis, as this focuses on what will happen to the financial results if a level of activity or volume fluctuates.

4.6 Summary

In this chapter we have considered the impact on cost and profit of changes in activity levels. You have drawn up a marginal cost statement and calculated the contribution of various products. You have considered the importance of limiting factors which may constrain the growth of an organisation and therefore affect the decision-making process. You have also used some general rules to calculate which is the more profitable product to produce when limiting factors are present. Finally, you have drawn a break-even graph and used it to find the break-even point as well as using a number of formulae.

Further reading

Bendrey, Mike, Hussey, Roger, West, Colston, *Accounting and Finance for Business Students*, DP Publications, 3rd Edition, 1994, Chapter 33.

Sizer, John, *Insight into Management Accounting*, Penguin, 1989, Chapter 5.

Watts, John, *Accounting in the Business Environment*, Pitman, 1993, Chapter 18.

Exercises

Progress questions

These questions have been designed to help you remember the key points in this chapter. The answers to these questions are given on page 94 at the back of this book.

Complete the following sentences:

1. When activity increases, fixed costs per unit ....

2. Marginal costing is a technique ....

3. Contribution is calculated by ....

4. The break-even point is where ....

5. The margin of safety is ....

Select the correct response to the following statements:

6. When activity increases, total variable costs increase.

    True ☐ False ☐

7. When activity decreases, total fixed costs decrease.

    True ☐ False ☐

8. When activity increases, fixed costs per unit increase.

    True ☐ False ☐

9. When activity decreases, fixed costs per unit increase.

    True ☐ False ☐

10. When activity increases, variable cost per unit stay the same.

    True ☐ False ☐

Review questions

These questions have been designed to help you check your comprehension of the key points in this chapter. You may wish to look further than the text in this chapter in order to answer them fully. You will find your library useful as a source of wider reading. You can check your answers by referring to the appropriate section.

11. Distinguish between the behaviour of fixed and variable costs when activity increases. (Section 4.2)

12. Explain the concept of contribution. (Section 4.3)

13. What is meant by 'the margin of safety'? (Section 4.4)

14. Why are limiting factors important? (Section 4.5)

Multiple choice questions

The answers to these questions will be given in the Lecturer's Supplement.

15. If the selling price per unit is £27.00 and the variable costs per unit are £13.00, the contribution per unit is:
    a)   £40.00
    b)   £14.00
    c)   £13.00
    d)   none of these

16. If the variable costs per unit are £6.00 and 500 units have been sold for £5,000, the total contribution is:
    a)   £4,000
    b)   £2,000
    c)   £3,000
    d)   £8,000

17. If the contribution per unit is £2.00 and the total variable costs for 100 units is £300, the total sales figure for those 100 units is:
    a)   £200
    b)   £500
    c)   £700
    d)   £100

18. If the total fixed costs are £12,000, the selling price per unit is £12 and the variable costs are £8 per unit, the break-even point is:
    a)   12,000 units
    b)   3,000 units
    c)   1,500 units
    d)   4,500 units

19. If fixed costs are £80,000 and contribution is 50p per unit, the number of units to be sold to achieve a target profit of £50,000 is:
    a)   60,000 units
    b)   260,000 units
    c)   600,000 units
    d)   200,000 units

Practice questions

A marking guide to these questions will be given in the Lecturer's Supplement.

20. Describe the circumstances in which you would use marginal costing to make a decision.

21. Explain the impact of limiting factors and how you would allow for them. Use a worked example to illustrate your answer.

22. A business has fixed costs of £1,000 and sells its product for £2.50 per unit. The variable costs are £1.20 per unit. Draw a break-even graph.

Questions for advanced students

A marking guide to these questions will be given in the Lecturer's Supplement.

23. What are the limitations of marginal costing?

24. Compare marginal costing and absorption costing.

Assignment: The Fair Play Company

A marking guide to this assignment will be given in the Lecturer's Supplement.

You are an assistant management accountant in a company which manufactures fairground equipment. The company uses absorption costing and like many other firms in recent years, has been suffering in the economic recession. Steve Wrench, the production manager, is worried because his total cost per unit is increasing despite the strict cost controls he exercises. Diane Flowers, the marketing manager, is complaining that in order to maintain sales volume, the selling price per unit must be reduced. They have had a meeting and calculated that the price Diane has suggested is lower than the total cost per unit as calculated by Steve. They have come to the conclusion that if they lower the price and increase their sales volume, it will lead to even larger losses.

Required

Write a report addressed to Mr Wrench and Ms Flowers explaining:

i) why the total cost per unit increases as production decreases;

ii) why marginal costing may be more appropriate than absorption costing for decision-making in times of recession.

5 Capital investment appraisal

5.1 Introduction

This chapter considers a number of techniques which can be used to make a decision when investing in a long-term capital project.

On completing this chapter you should be able to:

❐ appraise a capital investment project using a number of techniques;

❐ explain the advantages and disadvantages of the techniques;

❐ explain the importance of the concept of the time value of money;

❐ use discounted cash flow tables.

5.2 Purpose of capital investment appraisal

When a business is considering the investment of a large sum of money in a long-term project, the most important objective is to ensure that the money received over the life of the project is higher than the original investment. Therefore, the annual profit and the distinction between fixed and variable costs is of lesser importance than the timing and amount of the cash going in and out of the business.

In some cases an investment is made, not to generate more cash, but to make a saving on present costs. For example, a business may be deciding whether to replace a machine with a new model which is less expensive to run. The question is whether the savings in costs are sufficiently high to warrant the investment in the new machine. Once again, it is cash which is the most important factor.

Activity

A company has a choice between three machines, each costing £100,000 to purchase. Each machine will last for three years and the company estimates that over that period the positive net cash flows, that is the difference between the cash coming in and going out each year, will be as follows:

Year	Machine 1	Machine 2	Machine 3
	£	£	£
1	60,000	20,000	10,000
2	40,000	40,000	20,000
3	20,000	60,000	95,000

Which machine would you recommend the company purchases?

In order to make the comparison, you need to total the above cash flows:

Year	Machine 1 £	Machine 2 £	Machine 3 £
1	60,000	20,000	10,000
2	40,000	40,000	20,000
3	20,000	60,000	95,000
Total	120,000	120,000	125,000

Machines 1 and 2 both give the same total net cash inflow of £120,000 over the three-year period and therefore either would be a worthwhile investment. However, you may decide that machine 1 is preferable because the cash comes in more quickly. Machine 3 looks better than the other two because the total net cash inflow is £125,000. However, you have to wait until year 3 before you get most of the cash and this means that the risk is increased. With all three machines the company has estimated the cash flows and the further into the future the estimate is, the more unreliable it is likely to be. It is therefore difficult to decide which is the 'best' machine to buy and we need a specific technique to help us.

A number of different techniques of project appraisal are described in this chapter. Each has advantages and disadvantages and may give different answers to the same problem. Therefore, management must decide which is the most appropriate technique to use in the circumstances.

5.3 Payback period

Calculating the *payback period* is a simple technique for appraising the acceptability of projects and is very popular with non-accountants. The project is considered purely from the point of view of its cash flow over the life of the project. The objective is to recover the cash outlay in the shortest possible time.

Activity

You are considering buying an ice cream van, which will last for five years, and employing someone to operate it. Cash spent on buying the van would be £12,000. For each year the cash flows are estimated as follows:

	£	£
Cash in:		
Sales		20,000
Cash out:		
Purchases (ingredients)	5,000	
Wages for driver/salesperson	9,000	
Expenses (petrol, tax, insurance, repairs, etc.)	2,000	16,000
Net cash flow		4,000

Calculate the payback period.

You will see that depreciation of the van itself is not included because depreciation is not a cash flow. The cash flow relative to the van is the cash paid for van when we buy it. Check your answer against the following solution:

Year	Yearly net cash flows £	Cumulative net cash flows £
0	(12,000)	(12,000)
1	4,000	(8,000)
2	4,000	(4,000)
3	4,000	Nil
4	4,000	4,000
5	4,000	8,000

There are several things in this table which need explaining.

❏ Year 0 is a conventional way of saying start of year 1. Year 1, 2, 3, etc. means end of year 1, 2, 3, etc.

❏ It is customary to assume that cash flows during a year will be received at the end of that year. Of course, this is not true, but it simplifies the calculation and errs on the side of conservatism by giving a slightly pessimistic rather than an optimistic view if the cash flows are positive. It is possible to produce cash flows on a quarterly or monthly basis, but this is seldom done in payback calculations, because forecasting to this degree of refinement is rarely possible.

❏ Negative cash flows (cash going out) are shown in brackets, whereas positive cash flows (cash coming in) are not.

❏ The cumulative cash flows are shown as nil at the end of year 3. This means that at the end of year 3 the cash flowing in from the project has reached the figure of £12,000, which is same as the initial cash outflow in payment for the van at the start of year 1. Therefore, we can say that the payback period for the project is three years.

Activity

The net cash flows for a project have been budgeted as follows::

Year	Yearly net cash flows £
0	(18,000)
1	8,000
2	8,000
3	8,000
4	8,000
5	8,000

What is the payback period?

You need to work out the cumulative net cash flows over the period. Check your answer against the following:

Year	Yearly net cash flows £	Cumulative net cash flows £
0	(18,000)	(18,000)
1	8,000	(10,000)
2	8,000	(2,000)
3	8,000	6,000
4	8,000	14,000
5	8,000	22,000

The answer lies somewhere between two and three years. Assuming the cash flow is regular throughout the year, it should be easy to see that the answer is $2\frac{1}{4}$ years or two years and three months. If the figures are not simple, the way to calculate the part year is:

Year	Cumulative net cash flow
	£
2	(2,000)
3	6,000

Add the two cumulative cash flows ignoring the fact that the first figure is negative (in brackets):

$2,000 + 6,000 = 8,000$

Then divide the earlier figure (2,000) by the total:

$$\frac{2,000}{8,000} = \frac{1}{4} \text{ of a year}$$

Therefore the payback period is $2 + \frac{1}{4} = 2\frac{1}{4}$ years.

Activity

What do you consider are the advantages of the payback period technique?

The main advantages are as follows:

❐ The technique is very simple to calculate and is understood by managers who are not very numerate.

❐ It produces results which are useful for 'risky' projects, e.g. where the prediction of cash flows for more than the first few years is difficult, due, say, to possible changes in the market. For example, changes in technology may make a product obsolete in a year or so, although the current market for it seems assured.

❐ Some businesses may need to consider short-term cash flows more important than long-term cash flows, perhaps due to lack of capital adequate to sustain long-term objectives. It is not much use aiming for long-term profitability if the business fails in six months' time from lack of cash.

Activity

What do you consider are the disadvantages of the payback period technique?

The main disadvantages are as follows:

❐ Net cash inflows in year 5 are given the same degree of importance as those for year 1. Cash now or soon is worth more than the same amount of cash in five years' time. This is known as the *time value of money*.

❐ The technique ignores cash flows after the payback period.

Your answer should be machine 1 because this has a payback period of two years and the other machines are in excess of this. However, using the payback period would mean that we would not select machine 3, which gave the greatest return of cash. This is one of the disadvantages of the technique.

5.4 Accounting rate of return

Whereas the payback period method is concerned with cash flows, the *accounting rate of return* (ARR) is concerned with profit and average capital employed. Profit we will define as *profit before interest and tax*. The other figure used to calculate the accounting rate of return is *average capital employed*. Capital employed means the money that is tied up in the business and this can be defined as *fixed assets plus current assets less current liabilities*.

Average capital employed means that if the capital employed is £18,000 at the beginning of next year and £22,000 at the end of next year, then the average capital employed for next year is £20,000 (£18,000 plus £22,000 divided by 2 years). ARR is calculated as profit before interest and tax as a percentage of average capital employed:

$$\frac{\text{Profit before interest and tax}}{\text{Average capital employed}} \times 100$$

You should have calculated the figures needed for the formula before working it out:

	Project A	Project B
	£	£
Sales	62,000	109,000
Less Cost of sales	43,400	82,000
Profit before interest and tax	18,600	27,000

ARR:

$$\frac{\text{Profit before interest and tax}}{\text{Average capital employed}} \times 100 \qquad \frac{18,600}{100,000} \times 100 \qquad \frac{27,000}{180,000} \times 100$$

		= 18.6%	= 15%
Rank		1	2

If we rank these projects by their ARR, then project A has the higher ARR of 18.6% compared with 15% for project B.

However, Richard would be well advised not to base his decision purely on this method of project appraisal. For example, it would be interesting to know what the payback periods would be. We cannot calculate them because the information given is inadequate. Also, you can see that project B requires more capital than project A (an average of £180,000 compared with £100,000), but project B makes more profit than project A in absolute terms (£27,000 compared with £18,600).

Assuming that the capital required for project B is available for investment, then since project A requires less than half this amount, what is Richard to do with the difference? He could put it in a building society, but the return would be likely to be much less than the 15% for project B. How about investing in two projects of the A type? This could be considered, but it may not be possible. In other words, ARR is too poor a technique to be a satisfactory basis for a decision. It leaves too many questions unanswered.

Activity

What do you consider are the advantages of the accounting rate of return technique?

The main advantages are as follows:

❏ Calculations are very simple.

❏ The entire life of the project is taken into account.

Activity

What do you consider are the disadvantages of the accounting rate of return technique?

The main disadvantages are as follows:

❏ The timing of cash movements is completely ignored.

❏ There are a number of different definitions of accounting rate of return and various ways of calculating it which can lead to confusion.

- ❐ The crucial factor in investment decisions is cash flow and the accounting rate of return uses profits.
- ❐ The technique takes no account of the time value of money; a topic we discuss in the next section.
- ❐ It takes no account of the incidence of profits;
- ❐ Averages can be misleading.

5.5 Principles of discounted cash flow

In the previous section we said that the project appraisal techniques of payback and accounting rate of return take no account of the time value of money. The basic principle is that £1 received now is worth more than £1 received at some time in the future. One reason for this is that money received now can be invested.

Activity

If someone wanted to borrow money from you now and promised to pay you £100 in one year's time, how much would you be willing to lend them if the usual interest rate is 10%?

In answering this problem one concern you will have is whether you are likely to be paid the £100. If you consider it is doubtful, you may decide not to lend the money or, if you do, to charge a higher rate of interest because of the higher risk. If you consider the loan is safe, then you may be willing to lend £90.90. In a year's time this would give interest of £9.10 to make the sum of £100 which you are repaid.

Activity

How much would you be willing to lend now, if the interest rate is 15% and the borrower promises to repay £500 in 3 years' time?

You may have found this more difficult than the first question and you will have had to make some complex calculations to arrive at the correct answer of £329. However, there is an easy method if you turn to the *discounted cash flow tables* in the Appendix and look at Table 1 Present Value Factors. The question we are trying to answer is what is the *present value* of £500 received in three years' time, if the interest rates are 15%. If you look in the left hand column at 3 years and read across to the 15% column, you will see that the discount factor is 0.658. This is for £1, so we need to multiply this by £500. This gives the figure of £329 which is the amount you would be willing to lend now.

Activity

Check the above answer by working out 15% compound interest on £329 for three years.

Your answer should look like this:

	£
Principal	329.00
Interest Year 1	49.35
	378.35
Interest Year 2	56.75
	435.10
Interest Year 3	65.27
Total at end of three years	500.37

It is the above concept of the time value of money which underpins the two most sophisticated techniques in capital investment appraisal, *net present value* and *internal rate of return*, which we will look at next.

5.6 Net present value

Net present value (NPV) converts the future net cash flows into present day values and the project with the largest net present value is the one preferred. Many problems, both in real life and in exams, are concerned with choosing between alternatives, even if one alternative is to do nothing.

Activity

Keith Hacker is considering whether to buy a computer which will improve his cash flows by £30,000 per annum for the next five years, at the end of which time the computer will be out of date and of no value. The computer will cost £75,000 and will be bought for cash. The discount rate which Keith thinks is suitable is 15%.

Using the following pro forma and Table 1 Present Value Factors in the Appendix, calculate the net present value of this project.

Year	Detail	Cash flows £	Discount factor at 15%	Present value £
0	Purchase of computer	(75,000)	1.000	(75,000)
1	Net cash inflow			
2	Net cash inflow			
3	Net cash inflow			
4	Net cash inflow			
5	Net cash inflow			
	Net present value:			

If you had problems with this activity, you may find the following comments helpful.

- ❑ The purchase of the computer is a negative cash flow and is shown in brackets. The discount factor is 1.000 because the cash outflow is at year 0.
- ❑ It is assumed that the cash flow always takes place at the end of the year.

The solution is as follows:

Year	Detail	Cash flows £	Discount factor at 15%	Present value £
0	Purchase of computer	(75,000)	1.000	(75,000)
1-5	Net cash inflow	30,000	3.352	100,560
	Net present value:			25,560

You should have got the same NPV of £25,560, but you will see that we have taken a short cut. The discount factor of 3.352 can be found in Table 2 Cumulative Present Value Factors, and is used to save the effort of multiplying £30,000 in turn by the individual figures from Table 1 for years 1 to 5 inclusive. You can only use this short cut when it is the same amount of cash each year, otherwise you must use Table 1.

The net present value of the project is a positive £25,560. It is called net because the initial outlay on the machine has been deducted from the total of the discounted inflows. Since the project has a positive NPV, Keith will be getting a return on his investment of more than 15%. If the NPV had been nil, his return would be 15%. If the project had shown a negative NPV, the return would be less than 15%, and it would not therefore be worth undertaking.

5.7 Internal rate of return

The *internal rate of return (IRR)* uses the same principles as NPV, but the aim is to find the discount rate which gives a net present value of 0 for the project. In other words, the aim of the technique is to show the percentage return you obtain on the investment.

Activity

In the above example we concluded that at a discount rate of 15%, a positive NPV of £25,560 made Keith's investment worthwhile. In other words Keith would be getting a return on the project in excess of 15%. Using the following pro forma, and Discount Table 2 in the Appendix, recalculate the NPV, using discount rates of 20%, 25% and 30%.

			At 20%		At 25%		At 30%	
Year	Cash flows £	Discount factor	Present value £	Discount factor	Present value £	Discount factor	Present value £
0	(75,000)	1.000	(75,000)	1.000	(75,000)	1.000	(75,000)
1-5	30,000						

Check your answer against the following:

Year	Cash flows £	At 20% Discount factor	At 20% Present value £	At 25% Discount factor	At 25% Present value £	At 30% Discount factor	At 30% Present value £
0	(75,000)	1.000	(75,000)	1.000	(75,000)	1.000	(75,000)
1-5	30,000	2.991	89,730	2.689	80,670	2.436	73,080
			14,730		5,670		(1,920)

The information we now have can be summarised as follows:

❏ At a discount rate of 15%, the NPV is a positive £25,560.

❏ At a discount rate of 20%, the NPV is a positive £14,730.

❏ At a discount rate of 25%, the NPV is a positive £5,760.

❏ At a discount rate of 30%, the NPV is a negative £1,920.

Looking at this, you can see that the higher the discount rate, the smaller the NPV becomes, until it eventually becomes negative somewhere between 25% and 30%. The IRR lies at the point where the NPV changes from positive to negative, i.e. where it is nil.

This can be illustrated by plotting the NPVs on a graph against the appropriate discount rates. The discount rates are marked on the x axis, and NPVs on the y axis.

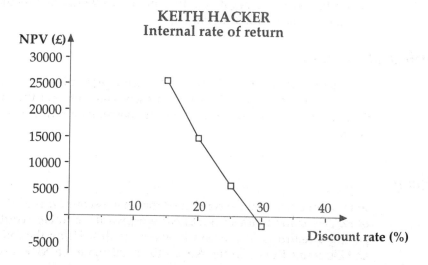

KEITH HACKER
Internal rate of return

You will see that the line joining the four points is a slight curve, but for all practical purposes, we can assume that it is a straight line, provided the points are not too far apart. We shall use the data at 25% and 30% discount rates. The discount rate at which the line crosses the x axis, where NPV is nil, is somewhere between 25% and 30%, i.e. 25 plus a number between 0 and 5 (30 - 25).

The calculation involves *linear interpolation*, (linear, because it assumes a straight line), and is as follows:

$$25 + 5 \times \left[\frac{5,670}{5,670 + 1,920} \right] = 28.7\%$$

The calculation shows that Keith will get a return of 28.7% on the project. The figures in square brackets represent the proportion of 5 which we require to be added to 25:

$$\frac{\text{NPV of 25\% rate}}{\text{NPV of 25\% rate} + \text{NPV of 30\% rate}}$$

We ignore the fact that the NPV of the 30% rate (£1,920) is negative, ie that the difference (or distance) between 5,670 and (1,920) is the total of the two figures, ignoring the fact that the second figure is negative. If you find this difficult to understand, the following explanations may help.

If yesterday you had £100 in the bank (positive figure), and today find you have an overdraft of £50 (negative figure), how much money have you drawn out of the bank since yesterday? The answer is £100 + £50 = £150

Activity

What do you consider are the advantages of the net present value and internal rate of return techniques?

The main advantages are as follows:

❏ They use the concept of the time value of money.

❏ The entire life of the project is taken into account.

❏ They permit comparisons with other opportunities to be made.

❏ They enable the organisation to decide on its financing policy.

Activity

What do you consider are the disadvantages of the net present value and internal rate of return techniques?

The main disadvantages are as follows:

❏ The calculations are complex.

❏ It is difficult to decide what is the most appropriate discount rate to use.

❏ Managers may have difficulty in understanding the technique.

5.8 Information required for discounted cash flow techniques

Although net present value and internal rate of return are useful techniques, they are also complex and managers may have difficulty in understanding the results. Since the main purpose of management accounting is to help managers by providing useful information, if the information presented is hard to interpret it makes less useful. As well as managers having problems in understanding the results of the calculations, the management accountant may have problems in obtaining the figures to do the calculations. These problems are common to all investment appraisal techniques based on cash flows.

Activity

What sort of problems do you think might be associated with investment appraisal techniques based on cash flows?

One major problem is concerned with *predicting the amount of cash* that is likely to come in and go out of the business over the life of the project. Some projects last for many years and it is impossible to forecast the amounts with certainty. For this reason many companies prefer the payback period, because it is based on the earliest cash flows. One cash flow which can arise at the end of a project is the sale of the machinery and equipment which was originally purchased for the project. With a large investment in machinery, the second-hand or scrap value may be very high, even after many years of use. The expected proceeds from the sale of any such assets must be shown as a cash inflow in the calculations.

Another problem which has not yet been mentioned is the *choice of discount factor*. In this chapter we have used a discount rate of 10% or 15%, but in practice management, with advice from the management accountant, must decide which rate to use. You will appreciate that the choice of discount factor is critical to the results of the calculation. One basis on which to choose the discount rate is to use the current rate of return the organisation receives on capital employed. Another method is to use the current cost of capital. Alternatively, the return on other projects available could be used or the rate which could be received if the organisation invested the capital externally.

When answering questions on capital appraisal, it is easy for students to concentrate on the calculations and forget these other aspects. The calculations are relatively easy, but the above issues make capital investment appraisal techniques complex. However, it is vital that the management accountant makes use of them, as they assist management in determining the likely return they will get from a long-term project and deciding whether it is acceptable in view of the risks involved.

5.9 Summary

In this chapter you have used the two techniques of project appraisal, payback period and accounting rate of return and considered their advantages and disadvantages. The payback period technique is concerned with cash flows and calculates the time it will take to recover the cash invested in the project. The accounting rate of return is concerned with profit and expresses this as a percentage of the average capital employed in the project. You also looked at discounted cash flow and the concept of the time value of money. You saw how this concept was used in the techniques of net present value and internal rate of return, and applied them to decision making.

Further reading

Bendrey, Mike, Hussey, Roger, West, Colston, *Accounting and Finance for Business Students*, DP Publications, 3rd Edition, 1994, Chapters 36,37,38 and 39.

Drury, Colin, *Costing: An Introduction*, Chapman & Hall, 1990, Chapter 14.

McLaney, E. J., *Business Finance for Decision Making*, Pitman, 1993, Chapter 3.

Exercises

Progress questions

These questions have been designed to help you remember the key points in this chapter. The answers to these questions are given on page 94 at the back of this book.

Complete the following sentences:

1. Payback technique has the disadvantage of ignoring ....

2. Accounting rate of return is calculated as ....

3. The time value of money concept ....

4. Positive net cash flow is ....

5. The aim of the internal rate of return is to ....

Select the correct response to the following statements:

6. With the accounting rate of return, the cash flows of the project are taken into account.

    True ☐ False ☐

7. The payback period takes account of the time value of money.

    True ☐ False ☐

8. Payback technique is good for high risk projects.

    True ☐ False ☐

9. If a project has a positive net present value, it is not worth undertaking.

    True ☐ False ☐

10. In capital investment appraisal, cash is more important than profit.

    True ☐ False ☐

Review questions

These questions have been designed to help you check your comprehension of the key points in this chapter. You may wish to look further than the text in this chapter in order to answer them fully. You will find your library useful as a source of wider reading. You can check your answers by referring to the appropriate section.

11. What are the main advantages and disadvantages of the payback period technique? (Section 5.3)

12. How would you calculate the accounting rate of return? (Section 5.4)

13. What is meant by the time value of money? (Section 5.5)

14. Explain the calculation for linear interpolation. (Section 5.7)

Multiple choice questions

> *The answers to these questions will be given in the Lecturer's Supplement.*

15. Payback period is the time in years which it takes for cash inflows of a project to equal:

   a) the average capital employed
   b) the cost of capital employed
   c) the cash overdraft limited agreed with the bank
   d) the cash outflows

16. A project has a cash outflow in year 0 of £17,100 and cash inflows for the first and subsequent years of £3,600 per annum. The payback period is:

   a) $4\frac{1}{4}$ years
   b) $4\frac{3}{4}$ years
   c) $4\frac{1}{2}$ years
   d) 4 years $7\frac{1}{2}$ months

17. The average profit before tax for the next three years of a project is budgeted at £8,500 per annum. The average capital employed over the three years is budgeted at £50,000. The ARR is:

   a) 17%
   b) 58%
   c) 51%
   d) 19.33%

18. Using a 18% rate of discount, the present value of £753 to be received in 10 years' time is:

   a) £38.00
   b) £380.00
   c) £37.00
   d) £3.70

19. A project has the following cash flows:

Year	Cash flows
	£
0	(20,000)
1	10,000
2	10,000
3	10,000

   Using a 15% discount rate, the NPV is:

   a) £22,830
   b) £2,830
   c) £283
   d) (£2,830)

Practice questions

> *A marking guide to these questions will be given in the Lecturer's Supplement.*

20. Explain why the payback period is preferable to the account rate of return.

21. What are the advantages and disadvantages of using discounted cash flow?

22. Describe the procedures for calculating the net present value of a project.

Questions for advanced students

> *A marking guide to these questions will be given in the Lecturer's Supplement.*

23. What issues should be considered when deciding the discount factor?

24. Compare the net present value with the internal rate of return.

Assignment: Melrose Conferences

A marking guide to this assignment will be given in the Lecturer's Supplement.

Kerry Melrose has a conference organising business and is thinking of buying some computer controlled audio visual equipment. She has done her calculations on a cash basis and has discovered that the equipment will cost £10,000. At the end of the first year she will have to spend £5,000 on training and advertising, and this should generate an additional £1,000 worth of business. In the second year, she estimates that the advertising costs will reduce to £3,000, but an additional £2,000 worth of business will be generated. In the third and fourth years no advertising will be required and the additional business generated will be £3,000 in year 3 and £8,000 in year 4.Kerry believes that by the end of year 5 the equipment will be out of date, but she should be able to generate a further £6,000 worth of business in that year and be able to sell the equipment at the end of the year for £4,000.

Required

Write a report for Kerry Melrose which shows:

i) the payback period of the project

ii) the net present value of the project using a discount rate of 12%

iii) an explanation of the two techniques and an interpretation of their results

iv) your recommendation as to whether Kerry should go ahead with the project and any financial considerations she should bear in mind.

6 Budgetary control

6.1 Introduction

This chapter introduces the technique of budgetary control which is a method of financial control which compares planned and actual income and expenditure in an organisation.

At the end of this chapter you should be able to:

❐ identify the main features of a budgetary control system;

❐ describe the requirements for an effective system of budgetary control;

❐ list the advantages and disadvantages of a budgetary control system.

6.2 Business planning

The importance of *business planning* can be shown by looking at an example. Cascade (UK) plc manufactures bathroom fittings. Based on past production records, the production manager believes that 15,000 shower units will be needed and buys all the materials and stores them in a warehouse. The marketing manager has heard that the water companies are considering adopting a metered water system, based on usage, rather than a system of water rates based on property value, and has therefore launched a massive sales campaign. He believes that 30,000 shower units will be sold. The financial accountant has received a letter from the bank stating that overdraft facilities will be withdrawn. He has therefore decided to stop any expenditure which is not absolutely necessary. The designer has come up with a new design using recycled water. The personnel manager believes that the recession will get worse and has started issuing redundancy notices to the workforce.

This example illustrates how a lack of co-ordination of the various activities, and managers following their own ideas, can lead to resources not being matched to the demands made on them and result in waste and inefficiency. This is remedied by business planning. The first stage of business planning is for the owners or directors of the business to set out their *assumptions* of what is going to happen to the organisation's markets and business environment. Non-trading organisations also operate in a business environment and planning is just as crucial to them.

Activity

Make a list of the factors the owners or directors of an organisation should examine when arriving at their assumptions of what is going to happen to their markets and the business environment.

Depending on the type of organisation you were thinking of, the sort of factors you may have included are:

- ❏ changes in the size of the organisation's market and its anticipated share of the market;
- ❏ possible strategies of the organisation's competitors;
- ❏ likely changes in interest rates or sources of funding;
- ❏ likely cost increases and availability of energy, materials and labour;
- ❏ possibility of legislation or social pressures which will affect the organisation;
- ❏ effect of the activities of other related organisations;
- ❏ trends in climatic, demographic, environmental and other factors likely to affect the organisation's activities.

Having set out their assumptions, the owners or directors can then make *forecasts* about what is likely to happen in the year ahead. If they were to leave it at that, they would not be discharging their managerial responsibilities. For example, they might forecast that the organisation will become bankrupt. Although this may be accurate, it would clearly be unacceptable. They must find ways of minimising any threats to the organisation and taking advantage of any opportunities. By setting out the actions which must be taken in view of their predictions, they are making *business plans*.

The plans and policies established by the owners and directors must be converted into detailed plans covering all aspects of the organisation's activities. These are normally broken down on a monthly basis for a year or a longer period. Initially the plans may be in *quantitative terms*, for example the number of products to be made, the quantity of materials to be ordered. However, they will be converted into *financial terms* to form the *budgetary control system*. We will be looking at a formal definition of a *budget* in the next section, but at this stage we can consider a budget to be a plan expressed in financial terms covering a specified length of time. Next, the detailed plans must be translated into actions for each manager to pursue.

Activity

Using the example of Cascade (UK) plc again, both the production manager and the marketing manager need to know how many shower units they plan to sell in the coming year so that they can ensure that the number of shower units to be made will meet the anticipated demand. What suggestions would you make if either of the following circumstances arose?

i)   Many more shower units are made than can be sold.

ii)   Many more orders are received than the number of shower units made.

In the first situation you may have decided that it is necessary to cut back severely on production. This could lead to redundancies with machines and other resources not being used to their full capacity. Alternatively, you may have suggested that production continues at the same level and the excess production is stored, which could be very expensive. Finally, you may consider that the organisation should boost sales through price reductions or increased marketing. Both these options could also be very expensive.

In the second situation, although you may think that this is a good position for the business to be in, it can lead to considerable problems. If the company attempts to boost production, it may need overtime working at a higher wage rate. More machines and larger premises may be required, which may require taking out a loan to pay for them. If the company fails to meet the orders, customers will become dissatisfied and the firm's reputation will be harmed; customers may go to competitors where the service is better.

Whichever of the above alternatives the company chooses, the policy will have to be communicated to all managers. This will ensure that detailed plans can be drawn up which minimise the potential damage to the company's financial performance.

However, even if detailed plans are made available to all managers so that activities are co-ordinated, it does not mean that there is *control*. Because the plans are based on predictions, events will occur which mean that the plans cannot be achieved. Prices may rise unexpectedly; new competitors may enter the market and offer cheaper products; machines may break down; suppliers may not be able to deliver materials on time. If an organisation is going to achieve control, regular *monitoring* must take place so that what actually happens can be compared with the original plan. In this way action can be taken whenever circumstances dictate. The following diagram shows the process of business planning and monitoring which leads to budgetary control.

Business planning and control

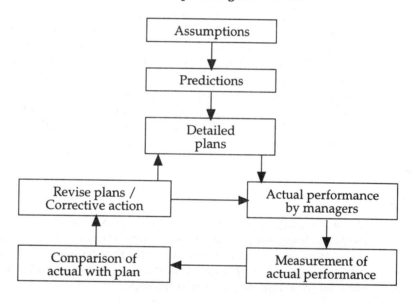

If there is no formal system of planning and control in an organisation, there will be an informal system. In small organisations, managers may be responsible for all the stages. In larger organisations, there is probably a formal system with a greater division of responsibility at each stage. Assumptions and predictions are normally made at board level following consultation throughout the organisation.

Collecting information to measure actual performance is part of the accounting function and accountants are also responsible for issuing financial statements which compare the actual performance with the plan. At this stage most managers find that they have a role in explaining any differences which have taken place between the plan and actual, and suggesting the appropriate course to pursue.

6.3 Purpose of budgetary control

As explained above, *budgetary control* is the setting of plans or budgets which lay down policies for which managers are responsible. A regular comparison is made of what is actually achieved with the plan, so that individual managers can remedy any divergence from the plan or revise the plan if necessary. The main *purpose* of *budgetary control* is to help managers in the planning and control of resources. However, there are a number of other purposes:

- ❏ A formal system of budgetary control enables an organisation to carry out its *planning* in a systematic and logical manner.

- ❏ *Control* can only be achieved by setting a plan of what is to be accomplished in a specified time period and managers regularly monitoring progress against the plan, taking corrective action where necessary.

- ❏ By setting plans, the activities of the various functions and departments can be *co-ordinated*. For example, the production manager can ensure that the correct quantity is manufactured to meet the requirements of the sales team, or the accountant can obtain sufficient funding to make adequate resources available to carry out the task, whether this is looking after children in care or running a railway network.

- ❏ A budgetary control system is a *communication system* which informs managers of the objectives of the organisation and the constraints under which it is operating. The regular monitoring of performance helps keep management informed of the progress of the organisation towards its objectives.

- ❏ By communicating detailed targets to individual managers, *motivation* is improved. Without a clear sense of direction, managers will become demotivated.

- ❏ By setting separate plans for individual departments and functions, managers are clear about their responsibilities. This allows them to *make decisions*, as long as they are within their budget responsibilities, and avoids the need for every decision to be made at the top level.

- ❏ By comparing actual activity for a particular period of time with the original plan any *variance* (difference), expressed in financial terms, is identified. This enables managers to assess their performance and decide what *corrective action*, if any, needs to be taken.

- ❏ By predicting future events, managers are encouraged to collect all the relevant information, analyse it and *make decisions* in good time.

- ❏ An organisation is made up of a number of individuals with their own ambitions and goals. The budgetary control process allows these individual goals to be modified and integrated with the overall objectives of the organisation. Thus, it encourages *consensus*. Managers can see how their personal aims fit into the overall context and how they might be achieved.

Activity

Give an example of a budget.

A cash *flow forecast* is a good example of a budget. You will have met this if you have done financial accounting. A cash flow forecast is a statement which shows the amount of cash which is expected to come in and go out during some period in the future. It is usually drawn up for each month over a 12 month period, and shows the monthly cash inflows and outflows, as well as the net cash flows and the cumulative cash position. A cash flow forecast is not a tool for control because it is only a plan. In order to achieve control, comparison must be made with the actual figures.

6.4 The budgetary control process

You will remember from Section 6.2 that a plan or budget is expressed in monetary terms and shows the income and/or expenditure needed during a financial period to achieve the given objective. However, in the first instance, the calculation may be carried out with quantities such as labour hours or kilos of materials. Budgets are drawn up for individual departments and functions, for example the sales budget and the production budget, as well as for capital expenditure, stock holding and cash flow. All the budgets are interrelated and incorporated into the *master budget*, which includes a budgeted profit and loss account and balance sheet. The following diagram shows the interrelationship of budgets in a simple organisation.

Interrelationship of budgets

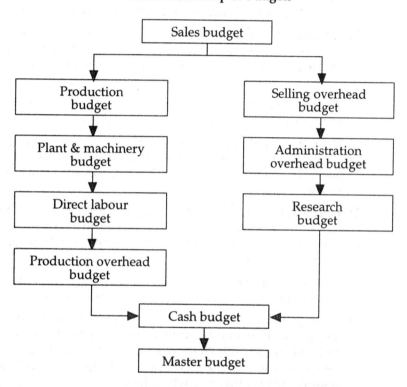

The following example shows how the budgets are linked. Portalight Limited manufactures torches. The sales director has estimated that the following quantities will be sold over the next 6 months:

	Jan	Feb	Mar	Apr	May	Jun
Sales	1,000	1,200	1,500	1,600	1,600	1,750

The production department will manufacture the torches in the month before the sales take place and it has been agreed that a buffer stock of 200 torches will be maintained. On December 1st there is a stock of 100 units.

Activity

How many torches must the production department manufacture each month?

The best way to tackle a problem of this nature is to draw up a table giving all the information:

	Dec	Jan	Feb	Mar	Apr	May	Jun
Opening stock	100	1,200	1,400	1,700	1,800	1,800	1,950
Production	1,100	1,200	1,500	1,600	1,600	1,750	
Sales		1,000	1,200	1,500	1,600	1,600	1,750
Closing stock	1,200	1,400	1,700	1,800	1,800	1,950	

Activity

Having calculated the number of torches which must be produced, what decisions must the production manager now take and which budgets will be affected?

The most immediate decisions the production manager needs to make concern whether there is sufficient machine capacity to make the torches and whether there is sufficient labour. It may be that more machines and labour are required in the busy months and more space will be required in the factory; therefore all these budgets will be affected.

The accountant will be concerned with the cash requirements for any changes and will want to ensure that the implications of these decisions are shown in the cash budget. It is because of the interrelated nature of budgets that a change in any one can affect all the other budgets.

The process of preparing budgets for each of the functions and other activities in an organisation and drawing up a *master budget* can take a number of months. The budgets must be communicated to managers before the start of the appropriate financial period, called the *budget period,* so that they know what the plans are for their own departments and can implement them.

Some organisations adopt the *top down approach* to budget setting: the owners or directors decide the individual plans for each department and function, and these plans are given to the individual managers to implement. Other organisations use the *bottom up approach* to budget setting: individual managers construct their own budgets which are given to the owners or directors who co-ordinate the individual budgets into a master budget. These are the two extremes and most organisations fall somewhere between the two.

A *budget committee* may be formed in the organisation which is made up of the functional or departmental managers and chaired by the chief executive. The management accountant usually occupies the role of committee secretary, co-ordinating and assisting in the preparation of the budget data provided by each of the managers. The budget committee reviews the budgets submitted by individual managers and ensures that each has the following characteristics:

❏ The budget conforms to the policies formulated by the owners or directors.

❏ It shows how the objectives are going to be achieved and recognises any constraints under which the organisation will be operating.

❏ It is realistic.

❏ It integrates with the other budgets.

❏ It reflects the responsibilities of the manager concerned.

If a budget does not display all these characteristics, it will need to be revised. This may affect other budgets and there may need to be negotiations between the managers concerned to introduce the necessary budget changes. When the budgets have been approved by the budget committee, they are submitted to the directors for approval prior to the commencement of the budget period. If the directors accept the budget, it is then adopted by the organisation as a whole and becomes the working plans.

There are a number of different types of budgets. A *fixed budget* is not changed even when actual activity levels differ from those set. A *flexible budget* is one which is changed to allow for the behaviour of variable costs at different levels of budgeted and actual activity. We shall be looking at flexible budgets in more detail in section 6.6.

6.5 Variance analysis

Variance analysis is the investigation of the factors which have caused the differences between the actual and the budgeted figures. The differences are known as *variances*. Actual progress is measured from the beginning of the budget period, which is usually a year. Each month the actual figures are compared with the plan and reported to the managers responsible.

If the actual costs are lower than the budgeted costs, there will be a *favourable variance* and this will result in a higher final profit. But if the actual costs are higher than the budgeted costs, the variance is known as an *adverse variance* which will result in a lower profit. There may also be income variances. If actual income is higher than budgeted income, there will be a *favourable variance* and this will result in a higher final profit. On the other hand, if actual income is lower than budgeted income, there will be an *adverse variance* which will result in a lower final profit. Adverse variance figures are usually shown in brackets.

Activity

Richard Pillinger, who we met in Chapter 5, has now made up his mind and has decided to invest in a small farming project in Jersey. The farm produces early tomatoes, green beans and cucumbers. Complete the following budget report by filling in the variances.

Budget report for May

	Budget	Actual	Variance
	£	£	£
Income:			
Early tomatoes	25,000	24,500	
Green beans	18,000	17,200	
Cucumbers	19,000	19,600	
Subtotal	62,000	61,300	
Costs:			
Salaries	28,400	29,000	
Expenses	12,500	12,000	
Administration	1,800	1,700	
Miscellaneous	700	300	
Subtotal	43,400	43,000	
Profit	18,600	18,300	

You should not have had too much difficulty in calculating the variances as it is simply a matter of subtracting the actual figures from the budgeted figures. Check your answer against the completed budget report below, making sure that you have remembered to show the adverse variances in brackets.

Budget report for May

	Budget £	Actual £	Variance £
Income:			
Early tomatoes	25,000	24,500	(500)
Green beans	18,000	17,200	(800)
Cucumbers	19,000	19,600	600
Subtotal	62,000	61,300	(700)
Costs:			
Salaries	28,400	29,000	(600)
Expenses	12,500	12,000	500
Administration	1,800	1,700	100
Miscellaneous	700	300	400
Subtotal	43,400	43,000	400
Profit	18,600	18,300	(300)

The budget report shows that in May, Richard made a profit which was £300 lower than planned. This was due to lower income from sales of early tomatoes and green beans than planned, combined with higher salaries paid. Now he must decide whether these adverse variances require any action on his part. The salary increase may not have been planned but is nevertheless necessary. The lower sales income may be due to factors beyond his control, such as unexpected bad weather affecting yield. Most businesses experience peaks and troughs during the year, especially where there are seasonal factors which affect production and demand, and these need to be reflected in the monthly budget figures. On the other hand, Richard may discover it is due to poor marketing or distribution problems. Before he can decide what action, if any, to take to remedy the adverse variances, Richard must first investigate the cause.

6.6 Fixed and flexible budgets

A *fixed budget* is a budget which is not changed once it has been established, regardless of changes in activity level. It may be revised if the situation so demands, but a fixed budget is not changed solely because the actual activity level differs from the budgeted activity level. This can be a considerable disadvantage because a fixed budget may show an adverse variance on costs which is simply due to an increase or decrease in variable costs. As you will remember from Chapter 4, total variable costs increase or decrease in proportion with changes in activity level.

A *flexible budget* changes in accordance with activity levels and reflects the different behaviours of fixed and variable costs. Therefore, in a flexible budget, any cost variance can be assumed to be due to an increase or decrease in fixed costs. A flexible budget may be used at the planning stage to illustrate the impact of achieving different activity levels. It can also be used at the control stage at the end of a month to compare the actual results with what they should have been.

The following example shows the importance of flexible budgeting. Portalight Limited's budget for January is based on an output of 1,000 torches. The following budget report shows the budgeted and actual figures for the month when 1,100 torches were sold.

Portalight Limited
Budget report for January

	Budget		Actual	
	£	£	£	£
Sales		1,500		1,650
Variable costs	750		880	
Variable overheads	250		260	
Fixed overheads	200		200	
Total costs		1,200		1,340
Profit		300		310

The managing director has been sent the above budget statement and is delighted that the actual profit is £10 above the budget.

Activity

Write a report to the managing director explaining why he should not be so pleased with the results. Support your report with calculations.

After all the work you have done on marginal costing in Chapter 4, the words 'variable costs' should immediately have alerted you to the problem of comparing the actual results with the original budget when there has been a change in activity level. In this case the number of torches sold was 1,100, compared with the planned amount of 1,000. Although the sales department must be congratulated on achieving increased sales, the company needs to construct a flexible budget to see if they have controlled their variable costs. This is done by multiplying the planned variable costs per unit by the actual level of production.

The variable costs were originally set at £750 for 1,000 torches, which is 75p per torch. The variable overheads were originally set at £250 for 1,000 torches, which is 25p per torch. If we assume that as the number of torches manufactured increases, the total variable costs increase, the flexible budget compared with the actual results is as follows:

Portalight Limited
Budget report for January

	Flexible budget		Actual	
	£	£	£	£
Sales (at £1.50 per unit)		1,650		1,650
Variable costs (1,100 × 75p)	825		880	
Variable overheads				
(1,100 × 25p)	275		260	
Fixed overheads	200		200	
Total costs		1,300		1,340
Profit		350		310

The flexible budget shows that at an output of 1,100 torches, a profit of £350 should have been made. A comparison of the figures shows that although variable overheads have been reduced, there is an overspend on variable costs which should be investigated.

6.7 Advantages and disadvantages of budgetary control

In this chapter we have described the way in which a budgetary control system is operated and the use of flexible budgets, but there is no single model of a perfect budgetary control system. Every organisation needs a system which meets its own particular needs. However, it is possible to list the requirements for a system to operate effectively.

> *Activity*
>
> What features do you consider should be present in an organisation for an effective system of budgetary control to be implemented?

If you have understood the chapter so far, you should have been able to list a number of features. These are the main items you should have considered:

- ❐ A sound and clearly defined organisation with the managers' responsibilities clearly indicated.
- ❐ Effective accounting records and procedures which are understood and applied.
- ❐ Strong support and the commitment of top managers to the system of budgetary control.
- ❐ The education and training of managers in the development, interpretation and use of budgets.
- ❐ The revision of the original budgets where circumstances show that amendments are required to make them appropriate and useful.
- ❐ The recognition throughout the organisation that budgetary control is a management activity and not an accounting exercise.
- ❐ An information system which provides data for managers so that they can make realistic predictions.
- ❐ The correct integration of budgets and their effective communication to managers.
- ❐ The setting of budgets which are reasonable and achievable.
- ❐ The participation of managers in the budgetary control system.

Sometimes management implements a system of budgetary control, but becomes disillusioned with it; the disadvantages seem to outweigh the advantages.

> *Activity*
>
> When an organisation has a budgetary control system, internal planning and control should be improved, which must be a considerable advantage. What other advantages might there be?

You may have thought of some of the following:

- ❐ Decisions are based on the examination of future problems in sufficient time for the organisation to take corrective action.

- ❒ With clearly defined objectives and the monitoring of achievement, motivation of the entire management team is improved.
- ❒ Plans can be reviewed regularly in the light of changing circumstances and can be amended where appropriate.
- ❒ The resources of the organisation are given the fullest and most economical use.
- ❒ The activities of all the various functions in the organisation are properly co-ordinated.
- ❒ Capital and effort are put to the most profitable use.

Activity

What do you consider are the disadvantages of a budgetary control system?

There are quite a number of potential drawbacks with a budgetary control system. How damaging they are depends on the way the system is operated. Disadvantages which might arise include the following.

- ❒ The process of drawing up budgets is time consuming and managers may be deflected from their prime responsibilities of running the organisation.
- ❒ The future is always uncertain and budgets may be unrealistic. This can lead to poor control and the disillusionment of managers.
- ❒ Budgets may be imposed by top management with no consultation; consequently managers may feel demotivated.
- ❒ If a fixed budget is set and actual activity fluctuates from the planned level, the budget may become irrelevant.
- ❒ Managers may consider the budgets as 'being set in stone' and instead of taking effective and sensible decisions when the circumstances warrant it, may be constrained by the original budget

Activity

What do you consider the advantages are of a flexible budgetary control system over fixed budgeting?

Flexible budgeting provides clearer information to management for decision making and control purposes. By comparing the actual results with what should have been achieved at that level of activity, a more accurate measure is given.

6.8 Summary

In this chapter we have looked at the need for business planning and the entire cycle of planning and control in an organisation. You have examined the way in which budgets are established for separate functions and integrated into a master budget and considered what organisational factors are required to operate an effective system of budgetary control. Finally, you have looked at the advantages and disadvantages of budgetary control, and of using fixed and variable budgets.

Further reading

Drury, Colin, Costing: *An Introduction*, Chapman & Hall, 1990, Chapter 11.

Dyson, J. R., *Accounting for Non-Accounting Students*, Pitman, 1991, Chapters 10 and 16.

Harper, W., *Cost Accounting*, M&E Handbooks, Pitman, 1993, Chapter 13.

Hussey, Roger, *Cost and Management Accounting*, Macmillan Professional Masters, 1989, Chapter 18.

Exercises

Progress questions

These questions have been designed to help you remember the key points in this chapter. The answers to these questions are given on page 94 at the back of this book.

Complete the following sentences:

1. A budget is ....

2. A flexible budget is ....

3. A good example of a budget is ....

4. All individual budgets are incorporated into a ....

5. An adverse cost variance is ....

Select the correct response to the following statements:

6. For control to be achieved, regular monitoring of actual performance must take place.

    True ☐ False ☐

7. A fixed budget changes as activity levels change.

    True ☐ False ☐

8. A budget committee comprises all the accountants in an organisation.

    True ☐ False ☐

9. A variance is the difference between a predetermined and an actual figure.

    True ☐ False ☐

10. Once budgets have been set for a financial period, they should never be changed.

    True ☐ False ☐

Review questions

These questions have been designed to help you check your comprehension of the key points in this chapter. You may wish to look further than the text in this chapter in order to answer them fully. You will find your library useful as a source of wider reading. You can check your answers by referring to the appropriate section.

11. Why is business planning important? (Section 6.2)

12. What are the purposes of budgetary control? (Section 6.3)

14. Describe what is meant by 'variance analysis'. (Section 6.5)

13. What are the requirements for an effective system of budgetary control?

    (Section 6.7)

Multiple choice questions

The answers to these questions will be given in the Lecturer's Supplement.

15. Budgetary control is used in the following types of organisation:
    a) limited companies
    b) charities
    c) sole traders
    d) any organisation

16. Budget periods may be for:
    a) 1 year
    b) 1 month
    c) 1 week
    d) any period

17. Budgets are used for:
    a) motivation
    b) planning
    c) control
    d) all of these

18. The major drawback of fixed budgets is that:
    a) they are drawn up for a single level of activity only
    b) they cannot show the differences between budgeted and actual cost
    c) they can never be used for cost control purposes
    d) they are drawn up for short-term use only

19. Flexible budgets should only be used where:
    a) the actual level of activity is likely to fluctuate
    b) production and sales are equal
    c) costs are classified according to cost behaviour
    d) all variances are normally adverse

Practice questions

A marking guide to these questions will be given in the Lecturer's Supplement.

20. Describe the main features of a budgetary control system.

21. What are the advantages and disadvantages of a budgetary control system?

22. Distinguish between a fixed budget and a flexible budget.

Questions for advanced students

A marking guide to these questions will be given in the Lecturer's Supplement.

23. What behavioural aspects would you expect to be associated with a system of budgetary control?

24. A typical criticism of planning is that it is an inexact science. Discuss this in the context of a budgetary control system.

Assignment: Budgeting for failure

A marking guide to this assignment will be given in the Lecturer's Supplement.

The director of a small publishing company recently introduced a budgetary control system. An accountant was appointed who drew up budgets for the advertising and editorial departments based on the actual results for the last three years. At the end of the first month of the new financial period, the actual total revenue was higher than planned, but the total advertising department costs were higher than budgeted. The editorial department actual costs were the same as those budgeted and the actual profit for the period was higher.

On receiving the first month's results, the director threatened to dismiss the advertising manager for exceeding the budgeted costs. The advertising manager retaliated by saying that he would resign unless the budgetary control system was scrapped. The accountant left to join another company.

Required

You are an assistant in a firm of consultants who have been called in to advise the company. Prepare a preliminary report covering the following:

i) an analysis of the problems and how you think they have arisen;

ii) guidelines for the operation of a successful and effective budgetary control system;

iii) recommendations as to what action the director of the client company should take.

7 Standard costing

7.1 Introduction

This chapter introduces the technique of standard costing, which is a method of financial control which compares predetermined and actual costs, and may form part of the budgetary control system.

At the end of this chapter you should be able to:

❐ describe the technique of standard costing;

❐ calculate the direct material variances;

❐ calculate the direct labour variances;

❐ list the advantages and disadvantages of standard costing.

7.2 Setting standards

Standard costing is a system of financial control which is closely associated with *budgetary control*. Many organisations use both systems, although one can be used without the other. However, it is less common to find a standard costing system in operation without a budgetary control system being present.

Budgetary control is applied to departments, budget centres and the organisation as a whole, and is a technique which can be used in any organisation, whether it is a business, charity, university, hospital, etc. Standard costing is mainly applied to products and processes. Therefore it is a technique which is more commonly used in manufacturing organisations, although it may also be useful in service industries. As in a budgetary control system, it allows the comparison of predetermined levels of costs and income with the actual costs and income achieved. Any differences, which are called variances, can then be investigated. Managers within the organisation can be held responsible for these variances and, by analysing the reasons for the variances, control can be achieved.

The predetermined costs are known as *standard costs*. These are the costs which are incurred under defined working conditions. The standard cost is calculated from technical specifications, which give the quantity of materials, labour and other elements of cost required, and relate them to the prices and wages it is anticipated will be in place for the period in which the standard cost is to be used. It is usual to measure the time in which it is planned to complete a certain volume of work in *standard hours* or *standard minutes*. This means that a standard hour is a measure of production output rather than a measure of time.

Activity

A company has set 1 standard hour's production at 500 units. In a 7 hour day, 4,000 units are produced. What is this output in standard hours?

You will have needed to make the following calculation to answer this question:

$$\frac{4{,}000 \text{ units}}{500 \text{ units per standard hour}} = 8 \text{ standard hours production}$$

The type of standards used depends on the philosophy of the organisation. A standard may be defined as a measurable quantity established in defined conditions. Organisations can set *ideal standards* or *attainable standards*. Ideal standards are based on the best possible working conditions. However, it is attainable standards which are most widely used in industry.

Activity

Why do you think attainable standards are more popular than ideal standards?

The main reason is that attainable standards are based on realistic efficient performance and allow for problems such as machine breakdown, material wastage, etc. Although ideal standards are useful for management decision making, there is the risk that employees will be demotivated by the impossibility of achieving them.

7.3 Variance analysis

Variance analysis is the investigation of the factors which have caused the differences between the standard and actual results. As in budgetary control, these differences are known as variances. Any variances are analysed to reveal their constituent parts, so that sufficient information is available to permit management investigation. *Favourable variances* are those which improve the predetermined profit. *Adverse variances* are those which reduce the predetermined profit.

Activity

In the stitching department of Just Jackets Ltd a hundred pockets can be made in one standard hour. In an eight-hour day, 950 pockets are produced. Will this give rise to a favourable or adverse variance? Why is this?

The first step is to calculate how many pockets should be made in the eight-hour day:

100 units per standard hour × 8 actual hours = 800 standard hours production

Next you should have calculated the variance by subtracting the standard hours production (800) from the actual production (950) to arrive at a figure of 150.

This is a favourable variance because 150 more pockets are produced than the 800 planned.

Now we are ready to make this part of the standard costing system, by expressing the variance in financial terms.

7.4 Direct material variances

In a manufacturing organisation the *direct product costs* are normally *direct material* and *direct labour*. The reasons for over or under-spending on either of these costs is based on the following simple concept:

$$\text{Total cost} = \text{Quantity used} \times \text{Unit price}$$

The difference between standard and actual total cost must be due to variations in the quantity used, the unit price or a combination of both.

Predetermined standards are set both for the *usage level* of direct material for a given volume of production and the *price* allowed per unit of direct material. The price standards are based on the price per unit expected to be paid or budgeted for the level of purchases projected over the period for which the standard is to be applied.

In general, any price variance is regarded as the responsibility of the purchasing manager or buyer and variation in the volume or quantity of materials consumed is regarded as the responsibility of the production manager. However, due to the inter-dependence of price and usage, responsibilities may be difficult to assign.

The *direct material variance* is based on the following formula:

$$\text{Total direct material cost} = \text{Quantity used} \times \text{Price per unit}$$

Standards are set for the *quantity* of materials to be used for a specific volume of production and the *price* to be paid per unit of direct material. The total direct material variance is calculated by using the following formula:

$$(\text{Standard quantity used} \times \text{Standard price per unit}) - \left(\begin{array}{c}\text{Actual quantity} \\ \text{used}\end{array} \times \begin{array}{c}\text{Actual price} \\ \text{per unit}\end{array}\right)$$

Activity

Just Jacket Ltd has decided to extend its range and manufacture denim jackets. One jacket requires a standard usage of 3 metres of direct material which has been set at a standard price of £2.20 per metre. In the period, 80 jackets were made and 260 metres of material consumed at a cost of £1.95 per metre. Calculate the total direct material variance.

To answer this question you should have put the figures into the above formula. However, the first stage is to calculate the standard quantity of materials for the actual level of production. As 80 jackets were made, and the company planned to use 3 metres of denim per jacket, the standard quantity for that level of production is 240 metres. Substituting the figures in the formula:

$$(240 \text{ metres} \times £2.20) - (260 \text{ metres} \times £1.95) = £528 - £507$$

$$= £21 \text{ favourable variance}$$

The difference of £21 between the planned cost and the actual cost is a favourable variance because we have spent less on our materials than we planned for that level of production.

Although this information is useful, it needs to be more precise to enable the management to take any action required. The reason why actual material costs can differ from the planned material costs for a given level of production is due to two factors. Either we have used more or less materials than planned and/or we have paid more or less per unit of materials than we planned.

The total direct material variance can be divided into a *usage variance* and a *price variance* as shown in the following diagram.

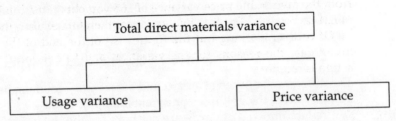

The usage *variance* is the difference between the standard quantity specified for the actual production and the actual quantity used at standard price per unit. The formula is:

(Standard quantity × Standard price per unit) – (Actual quantity × Standard price per unit)

Depending on the data you are given, you may find it more convenient to shorten this formula to the following:

(Standard quantity – Actual quantity) × Standard price per unit

Activity

Calculate the usage variance from the data for Just Jackets Ltd.

Once again, to answer this question you needed to insert the figures into the formula. The answer is:

(240 metres – 260 metres) × £2.20 = (£44.00) adverse variance

In this instance, there is an adverse variance because the company has used more material than planned for that level of production.

The final stage is to find out the *price variance*. This is the difference between the standard and actual purchase price per unit for the actual quantity of materials purchased or used in production. The formula is:

(Standard price per unit × Actual quantity) – (Actual price per unit × Actual quantity)

As with the usage variance, if the data is readily available, it may be more convenient to use the following shortened formula:

(Standard price per unit – Actual price per unit) × Actual quantity

Activity

Calculate the price variance from the data for Just Jackets Ltd.

The answer is:

(£2.20 - £1.95) × 260 metres = £65.00 favourable variance

The variance is favourable because we have paid less for the material than we planned for that level of production. If you deduct the adverse usage variance of £44 from the favourable price variance of £65 you obtain the total direct material variance of £21 favourable. The first two variances therefore explain the latter.

Of course, working out the figures is not the end of the task. Managers need to investigate the reasons for the variances and to determine whether any corrective action is required.

Activity

Jot down any reasons you can think of for the price and usage variances.

There are a number of reasons you could have suggested for the adverse usage variance. It may be that inferior materials were used and this led to higher wastage than planned. Perhaps the labour force was inexperienced and this led to high levels of wastage. Alternatively, some material may have been lost or stolen.

One strong possibility for the price variance is that the company has used poorer quality and therefore less expensive materials. This would tie in with the possible reason for the adverse usage variance. Other reasons may be that we are using a different supplier than originally intended or that we have negotiated a bulk discount.

7.5 Direct labour variances

The same principles apply to the calculation of the *direct labour variances* as you used for the direct material variances. Standards are established for the rate of pay to be paid for the production of particular products and the labour time taken for their production. The standard time taken is expressed in *standard hours* or *minutes* which becomes the measure of output. By comparing the standard hours allowed and the actual time taken, labour efficiency can be assessed. In practice, standard times are established by *work, time and method* study techniques.

The direct labour variance is based on the following formula:

Total labour cost = Hours worked × Rate per hour

The *total direct labour variance* is calculated by using the following formula:

(Standard direct labour hours × Standard rate per hour) – (Actual direct labour hours × Actual rate per hour)

The management of Just Jackets Ltd decides that it takes six standard hours to make one denim jacket and the standard rate paid to labour is £8 per hour. The actual production is 900 units and this took 5,100 hours at a rate of £8.30 per hour. Calculate the total direct labour hour variance.

With your knowledge of the calculation of material variances, this activity should have caused you few problems. The first stage is to calculate the standard direct labour hours for this level of production which is 900 jackets × 6 standard hours = 5,400 standard hours. The variance can then be calculated as follows:

(5,400 standard hours × £8.00) – (5,100 actual hours × £8.30)

$$=£43,200 - £42,330$$

$$= £870 \text{ favourable variance}$$

The variance is favourable because the total labour cost is less than we planned for that level of production. The total direct labour variance can be broken down into a *direct labour rate variance* and a *direct labour efficiency variance* as shown in the following diagram.

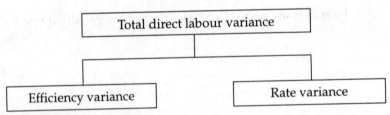

The direct labour efficiency variance is the difference between the actual production achieved, measured in standard hours, and the actual hours worked, valued at the standard labour rate. The formula is:

(Standard hours × Standard rate per hour) – (Actual hours × Standard rate per hour)

Depending on the data you have available, it may be more convenient to shorten the formula to:

(Standard hours – Actual hours) × Standard rate per hour

Calculate the direct labour efficiency variance.

The answer is:

(5,400 standard hours – 5,100 actual hours) × £8.00 = £2,400 favourable variance

The *direct labour rate variance* is the difference between the standard and actual direct labour rate per hour for the actual hours worked. The formula is:

(Standard rate per hour × Actual hours) – (Actual rate per hour × Actual hours)

Depending on the data you are given, you may find the following shortened formula more convenient:

(Standard rate per hour – Actual rate per hour) × Actual hours

The answer is:

(£8.00 – £8.30) × 5,100 actual hours = (£1,530) adverse variance

The variance is adverse because we have paid the workforce more than we planned for that level of production.

If you deduct the adverse direct labour rate variance of £1,530 from the favourable efficiency variance of £2,400, you get the favourable total direct labour variance of £870.

The most likely reason is that we have used more highly skilled labour than we originally planned. The rate we had to pay was therefore higher, but the output was greater than planned. There are other possible reasons; for example, we may have given a pay rise or overtime may have been worked. Further investigation would be required to identify the actual reasons and to determine whether any corrective action is required.

7.6 Advantages and disadvantages of standard costing

As with budgetary control, many of the benefits of standard costing are associated with the processes of planning. It compels managers to make decisions, co-ordinate activities and communicate with one another.

With your knowledge of budgetary control, you should not have had many problems with this activity. The main advantages are:

- ❑ Standard setting establishes a benchmark against which actual costs can be compared.
- ❑ The technique permits a thorough examination of the organisation's production and operations activities.
- ❑ As the standards are based on future plans and expectations, the information provided to management is much more accurate than that based merely on past performance.
- ❑ By examining the reasons for any variances between standard and actual costs and income, management needs only to concentrate on the exceptions to the planned performance. This leads to greater managerial efficiency.
- ❑ Variance analysis may result in cost reductions and control of costs is improved.

The main disadvantages are:

- ❑ It may be difficult to set standards, particularly in a new or dynamic organisation.
- ❑ The standard costing system may be expensive to maintain and the additional record keeping may become a burden to busy managers.
- ❑ Standards will naturally become out of date and require revision. In a very dynamic organisation this may happen so quickly that managers lose confidence in the system.
- ❑ Information provided by the system is only of value if it is used by managers for control purposes. If the information has no credibility or is not understood, it has no value.

7.7 Summary

In this chapter we have looked at standard costing and the calculation of variances. You have calculated variances for both total material costs and total labour costs. You have also calculated the sub-variances and considered the reasons why they have occurred. Finally, you have examined the advantages and disadvantages of a standard costing system.

Further reading

Bendrey, Mike, Hussey, Roger, West, Colston, *Accounting and Finance for Business Students*, DP Publications, 3rd Edition, 1994, Chapter 30.

Glautier, M. W. E. & Underdown, B., *Cost Accounting*, Pitman, 1988, Chapter 15.

Lucey, T., *Costing*, DP Publications, 1993, Chapters 24 and 25.

Exercises

Progress questions

These questions have been designed to help you remember the key points in this chapter. The answers to these questions are given on page 94 at the back of this book.

Complete the following sentences:

1. Ideal standards are based on ....

2. Variance analysis is the ....

3. Differences between standard and actual costs must be due to ....

4. A material price variance is the responsibility of ....

5. The sub-variances of the total direct material variance are ....

Select the correct response to the following statements:

6. If actual income is higher than planned the variance will be adverse.

   True ☐ False ☐

7. If actual cost is higher than planned the variance will be adverse.

   True ☐ False ☐

8. If more hours are worked than planned there will be a usage variance.

   True ☐ False ☐

9. The price variance is the difference between the standard price and the actual price per unit multiplied by the standard quantity.

   True ☐ False ☐

10. The rate variance is the difference between the standard and the actual direct labour rate per hour for the actual hours worked.

   True ☐ False ☐

Review questions

These questions have been designed to help you check your comprehension of the key points in this chapter. You may wish to look further than the text in this chapter in order to answer them fully. You will find your library useful as a source of wider reading. You can check your answers by referring to the appropriate section.

11. Compare ideal and attainable standards. (Section 7.2)

12. What is variance analysis? (Section 7.3)

13. What are the possible reasons for material usage variances? (Section 7.4)

14. What is meant by a standard hour? (Section 7.5)

Multiple choice questions

The answers to these questions will be given in the Lecturer's Supplement.

15. The formula for the material price variance is:
    a) (Standard price per unit – Actual price per unit) × Standard quantity
    b) (Standard quantity – Actual quantity) × Standard price per unit
    c) (Standard price per unit – Actual price per unit) × Actual quantity
    d) (Standard quantity – Actual quantity) × Actual price per unit

16. The formula for the material usage variance is:
    a) (Standard price per unit– Actual price) × Standard quantity
    b) (Standard quantity – Actual quantity) × Standard price per unit
    c) (Standard price per unit – Actual price per unit) × Actual quantity
    d) (Standard quantity – Actual quantity) × Actual price per unit

17. The formula for the labour efficiency variance is:
    a) (Standard rate per hour – Actual rate per hour) × Actual hours
    b) (Standard hours – Actual hours) × Actual rate per hour
    c) (Standard hours – Actual hours) × Standard rate per hour
    d) (Standard rate per hour – Actual rate per hour) × Standard hours

18. The formula for the labour rate variance is:
    a) (Standard rate per hour – Actual rate per hour) × Actual hours
    b) (Standard hours – Actual hours) × Actual rate per hour
    c) (Standard hours – Actual hours) × Standard rate per hour
    d) (Standard rate per hour – Actual rate per hour) × Standard hours

19. A favourable material price variance arises when:
    a) more materials are used than planned
    b) more is paid per unit of materials than planned
    c) less is paid per unit of materials than planned
    d) the quantity of materials used is less than planned

Practice questions

A marking guide to these questions will be given in the Lecturer's Supplement.

20. Calculate and suggest possible reasons for the materials price variance from the following data:

    Standard price per kilo is £4

    Standard usage per unit is 5 metres

    Actual price per kilo is £3

    Actual usage per unit is 5 metres

21. Calculate and suggest possible reasons for the materials usage variance from the following data:

    Standard price per tonne is £50

    Standard usage is 1,000 tonnes

    Actual price per tonne is £50

    Actual usage is 995 tonnes

22. Suggest possible reasons for either material or labour variances under a standard costing system.

Questions for advanced students

A marking guide to these questions will be given in the Lecturer's Supplement.

23. A manufacturing company has set a standard price for materials of £100 per kilo and anticipates that it will make 4 units from 1 kilo of materials. The actual production is 200 units and 52 kilos of materials are used at a price of £98 per kilo. Calculate all the material variances and discuss the possible reasons for them.

24. A company plans to make 10 units per hour and the standard rate per hour is set at £9. In a financial period 50 units are made and this takes 460 hours. The total labour cost for the period is £5,060. Calculate all the labour variances and discuss the possible reasons for them.

Assignment: Aphrodite Showers

A marking guide to this assignment will be given in the Lecturer's Supplement.

Four years ago, your Uncle Mike set up a small manufacturing company, Aphrodite Showers, in Cyprus which manufactures shower screens. There are two models: the Paphos, which is the standard model, and the Nicosia, the de luxe model. Both models are made from frosted glass and have an aluminium frame and fittings. The standard model has plain glass and silver satin finish to the frame and fittings. The de luxe model has an attractive design on the glass and a polished gold finish to the frame and fittings.

Once a year your Uncle Mike comes back to spend Christmas with you and your family. This year, knowing that you are studying management accounting on your course, he asks for your advice. He explains that despite a buoyant market and excellent sales figures, his profits have been very disappointing and he wants to embark on a cost cutting exercise. After discussions, you find that he does not operate a standard costing system and does not seem to know what it is. However, he is very keen to learn and as he is only staying a few days, asks you to write to him in Cyprus with full details. He also invites you to visit him for a holiday during the summer.

Required

Write your Uncle Mike a letter explaining the advantages of a standard costing system, how it may be implemented and the information he can expect to obtain.

Appendices

Appendix 1

Answers to progress questions

Chapter 1

1. Accounting is concerned with identifying, measuring, recording and communicating the economic transactions of organisations.

2. Financial accounting is concerned with the classification, measurement and recording of business transactions and the preparation of annual financial statements.

3. Management accounting is concerned with the use of financial and statistical techniques and methods to provide information to managers.

4. A management accountant provides information to managers to help them with their responsibilities of controlling, planning and decision making.

5. A qualified management accountant is normally a member of the Chartered Institute of Management Accountants.

6. False

7. False

8. False

9. True

10. True

Chapter 2

1. A cost unit can be defined as a quantitative unit of the product or service to which costs are allocated.

2. Direct costs can be identified with a specific product or saleable service.

3. In the short term, fixed costs tend to remain the same irrespective of changes in the level of activity.

4. The average cost per unit can be misleading if there are significant changes in activity levels.

5. Labour costing is closely related to the method of remuneration operated by the organisation.

6. False

7. True

8. False

9. True

10. True

Chapter 3

1. Cost apportionment is the sharing of overheads over a number of cost centres.

2. An overhead analysis allows the apportionment and allocation of overheads to cost centres.

3. The overhead absorption rate is the method for charging overheads to cost units.

4. The overheads for service cost centres must be apportioned to production cost centres.

5. The direct labour hour absorption rate is calculated by dividing the overheads for the cost centre by the total direct labour hours for that cost centre.

6. False

7. True

8. False

9. False

10. False

Chapter 4

1. When activity increases, fixed costs per unit decrease.

2. Marginal costing is a technique whereby only the variable or marginal costs of production are charged to cost units.

3. Contribution is calculated by deducting variable costs from sales.

4. The break-even point is where the business makes neither a profit nor a loss.

5. The margin of safety is the difference between the selected level of activity and the break-even point.

6. True

7. False

8. False

9. True

10. True

Chapter 5

1. Payback technique has the disadvantage of ignoring the time value of money and cash flows after the payback period.

2. Accounting rate of return is calculated as the return expressed as a percentage of the average capital employed.

3. The time value of money concept is concerned with calculating the present value of future cash flows.

4. Positive net cash flow is where the sum of the cash coming in is greater than the sum of the cash going out.

5. An adverse cost variance is one where the actual costs are higher than the planned costs.

6. False

7. False

8. True

9. False

10. True

Chapter 6

1. A budget is a plan expressed in financial terms covering a specified period of time.

2. A flexible budget is one which is changed to allow for the behaviour of variable costs at different levels of activity.

3. A good example of a budget is a cash flow forecast.

4. All individual budgets are incorporated into a master budget.

5. Standard costing is a technique which allows the comparison of predetermined levels of costs with the actual figures achieved.

6. True

7. False

8. False

9. True

10. False

Chapter 7

1. Ideal standards are based on the best possible working conditions.

2. Variance analysis is the investigation of the factors which have caused the differences between the standard and actual results.

3. Differences between standard and actual costs must be due to variations either in quantity used or unit price or both.

4. A material price variance is the responsibility of the purchasing manager.

5. The sub-variances of the total direct materials variance are the usage variance and the price variance.

6. False

7. True

8. False

9. False

10. True

Appendix 2

Table 1 – Present Value Factors

Future years	1%	2%	3%	4%	5%	6%	Rate of discount 7%	8%	9%	10%	11%	12%	13%	14%	15%	16%
1	0.990	0.980	0.971	0.962	0.952	0.943	0.935	0.926	0.917	0.909	0.901	0.893	0.885	0.877	0.870	0.862
2	0.980	0.961	0.943	0.925	0.907	0.890	0.873	0.857	0.842	0.826	0.812	0.797	0.783	0.770	0.756	0.743
3	0.971	0.942	0.915	0.889	0.864	0.840	0.816	0.794	0.772	0.751	0.731	0.712	0.693	0.675	0.658	0.641
4	0.961	0.924	0.889	0.855	0.823	0.792	0.763	0.735	0.708	0.683	0.659	0.636	0.613	0.592	0.572	0.552
5	0.952	0.906	0.863	0.822	0.784	0.747	0.713	0.681	0.650	0.621	0.594	0.567	0.543	0.519	0.497	0.476
6	0.942	0.888	0.838	0.790	0.746	0.705	0.666	0.630	0.596	0.565	0.535	0.507	0.480	0.456	0.432	0.410
7	0.933	0.871	0.813	0.760	0.711	0.665	0.623	0.584	0.547	0.513	0.482	0.452	0.425	0.400	0.376	0.354
8	0.924	0.854	0.789	0.731	0.677	0.627	0.582	0.540	0.502	0.467	0.434	0.404	0.376	0.351	0.327	0.305
9	0.914	0.837	0.766	0.703	0.645	0.592	0.544	0.500	0.460	0.424	0.391	0.361	0.333	0.308	0.284	0.263
10	0.905	0.820	0.744	0.676	0.614	0.558	0.508	0.463	0.422	0.386	0.352	0.322	0.295	0.270	0.247	0.227
11	0.896	0.804	0.722	0.650	0.585	0.527	0.475	0.429	0.388	0.350	0.317	0.287	0.261	0.237	0.215	0.195
12	0.887	0.789	0.701	0.625	0.557	0.497	0.444	0.397	0.356	0.319	0.286	0.257	0.231	0.208	0.187	0.168
13	0.879	0.773	0.681	0.601	0.530	0.469	0.415	0.368	0.326	0.286	0.258	0.229	0.204	0.182	0.163	0.145
14	0.870	0.758	0.661	0.578	0.505	0.442	0.388	0.341	0.299	0.263	0.232	0.205	0.181	0.160	0.141	0.125
15	0.861	0.743	0.642	0.555	0.481	0.417	0.362	0.315	0.275	0.239	0.209	0.183	0.160	0.140	0.123	0.108
16	0.853	0.728	0.623	0.534	0.458	0.394	0.339	0.292	0.252	0.218	0.188	0.163	0.142	0.123	0.107	0.093
17	0.844	0.714	0.605	0.513	0.436	0.371	0.317	0.270	0.231	0.198	0.170	0.146	0.125	0.108	0.093	0.080
18	0.836	0.700	0.587	0.494	0.416	0.350	0.296	0.250	0.212	0.180	0.153	0.130	0.111	0.095	0.081	0.069
19	0.828	0.686	0.570	0.475	0.396	0.331	0.277	0.232	0.195	0.164	0.138	0.116	0.098	0.083	0.070	0.060
20	0.820	0.673	0.554	0.456	0.377	0.312	0.258	0.215	0.178	0.149	0.124	0.104	0.087	0.073	0.061	0.051

Future years	17%	18%	19%	20%	21%	22%	Rate of discount 23%	24%	25%	26%	28%	30%	35%	40%	45%	50%
1	0.855	0.847	0.840	0.833	0.826	0.820	0.813	0.807	0.800	0.794	0.781	0.769	0.741	0.714	0.690	0.667
2	0.731	0.718	0.706	0.694	0.683	0.672	0.661	0.650	0.640	0.630	0.610	0.592	0.549	0.510	0.476	0.444
3	0.624	0.609	0.593	0.579	0.565	0.551	0.537	0.525	0.512	0.500	0.477	0.455	0.406	0.364	0.328	0.296
4	0.534	0.516	0.499	0.482	0.467	0.451	0.437	0.423	0.410	0.397	0.373	0.350	0.301	0.260	0.226	0.198
5	0.456	0.437	0.419	0.402	0.386	0.370	0.355	0.341	0.328	0.315	0.291	0.269	0.223	0.186	0.156	0.132
6	0.390	0.370	0.352	0.335	0.319	0.303	0.289	0.275	0.262	0.250	0.227	0.207	0.165	0.133	0.108	0.088
7	0.333	0.314	0.296	0.279	0.263	0.249	0.235	0.222	0.210	0.198	0.178	0.159	0.122	0.095	0.074	0.059
8	0.285	0.266	0.249	0.233	0.218	0.204	0.191	0.179	0.168	0.157	0.139	0.123	0.091	0.068	0.051	0.039
9	0.243	0.226	0.209	0.194	0.180	0.167	0.155	0.144	0.134	0.125	0.108	0.094	0.067	0.048	0.035	0.026
10	0.208	0.191	0.176	0.162	0.149	0.137	0.126	0.116	0.107	0.099	0.085	0.073	0.050	0.035	0.024	0.017
11	0.178	0.162	0.148	0.135	0.123	0.112	0.103	0.094	0.086	0.079	0.066	0.056	0.037	0.025	0.017	0.012
12	0.152	0.137	0.124	0.112	0.102	0.092	0.083	0.076	0.069	0.063	0.052	0.043	0.027	0.018	0.012	0.008
13	0.130	0.116	0.104	0.094	0.084	0.075	0.068	0.061	0.055	0.050	0.040	0.033	0.020	0.013	0.008	0.005
14	0.111	0.099	0.088	0.078	0.069	0.062	0.055	0.049	0.044	0.039	0.032	0.025	0.015	0.009	0.006	0.003
15	0.095	0.084	0.074	0.065	0.057	0.051	0.045	0.040	0.035	0.031	0.025	0.020	0.011	0.006	0.004	0.002
16	0.081	0.071	0.062	0.054	0.047	0.042	0.036	0.032	0.028	0.025	0.019	0.015	0.008	0.005	0.003	0.002
17	0.069	0.060	0.052	0.045	0.039	0.034	0.030	0.026	0.023	0.020	0.015	0.012	0.006	0.003	0.002	0.001
18	0.059	0.051	0.044	0.038	0.032	0.028	0.024	0.021	0.018	0.016	0.012	0.009	0.005	0.002	0.001	0.001
19	0.051	0.043	0.037	0.031	0.027	0.023	0.020	0.017	0.014	0.012	0.009	0.007	0.003	0.002	0.001	0.000
20	0.043	0.037	0.031	0.026	0.022	0.019	0.016	0.014	0.012	0.010	0.007	0.005	0.002	0.001	0.001	0.000

Table 2 – Cumulative Present Value Factors

Future years	1%	2%	3%	4%	5%	6%	Rate of discount 7%	8%	9%	10%	11%	12%	13%	14%	15%	16%
1	0.990	0.980	0.971	0.962	0.952	0.943	0.935	0.926	0.917	0.909	0.901	0.893	0.885	0.877	0.870	0.862
2	1.970	1.942	1.913	1.886	1.859	1.833	1.808	1.783	1.759	1.736	1.713	1.690	1.668	1.647	1.626	1.605
3	2.941	2.884	2.829	2.775	2.723	2.673	2.624	2.577	2.531	2.487	2.444	2.402	2.361	2.322	2.283	2.246
4	3.902	3.808	3.717	3.630	3.546	3.465	3.387	3.312	3.240	3.170	3.102	3.037	2.974	2.914	2.855	2.798
5	4.853	4.713	4.580	4.452	4.329	4.212	4.100	3.993	3.890	3.791	3.696	3.605	3.517	3.433	3.352	3.274
6	5.795	5.601	5.417	5.242	5.076	4.917	4.767	4.623	4.486	4.355	4.231	4.111	3.998	3.889	3.784	3.685
7	6.728	6.472	6.230	6.002	5.786	5.582	5.389	5.206	5.033	4.868	4.712	4.564	4.423	4.288	4.160	4.039
8	7.652	7.325	7.020	6.733	6.463	6.210	5.971	5.747	5.535	5.335	5.146	4.968	4.799	4.639	4.487	4.344
9	8.566	8.162	7.786	7.435	7.108	6.802	6.515	6.247	5.995	5.759	5.537	5.328	5.132	4.946	4.772	4.607
10	9.471	8.983	8.530	8.111	7.722	7.360	7.024	6.710	6.418	6.145	5.889	5.650	5.426	5.216	5.019	4.833
11	10.368	9.787	9.253	8.760	8.306	7.887	7.499	7.139	6.805	6.495	6.207	5.938	5.687	5.453	5.234	5.029
12	11.255	10.575	9.954	9.385	8.863	8.384	7.943	7.536	7.161	6.814	6.492	6.194	5.918	5.660	5.421	5.197
13	12.134	11.348	10.635	9.986	9.394	8.853	8.358	7.904	7.487	7.103	6.750	6.424	6.122	5.842	5.583	5.342
14	13.004	12.106	11.296	10.563	9.899	9.295	8.745	8.244	7.786	7.367	6.982	6.628	6.302	6.002	5.724	5.468
15	13.865	12.849	11.938	11.118	10.380	9.712	9.108	8.559	8.061	7.606	7.191	6.811	6.462	6.142	5.847	5.575
16	14.718	13.578	12.561	11.652	10.838	10.106	9.447	8.851	8.313	7.824	7.379	6.974	6.604	6.265	5.954	5.668
17	15.562	14.292	13.166	12.166	11.274	10.477	9.763	9.122	8.544	8.022	7.549	7.120	6.729	6.373	6.047	5.749
18	16.398	14.992	13.754	12.659	11.690	10.828	10.059	9.372	8.756	8.201	7.702	7.250	6.840	6.467	6.128	5.818
19	17.226	15.678	14.324	13.134	12.085	11.158	10.336	9.604	8.950	8.365	7.839	7.366	6.938	6.550	6.198	5.877
20	18.046	16.351	14.877	13.590	12.462	11.470	10.594	9.818	9.129	8.514	7.963	7.469	7.025	6.623	6.259	5.929

Future years	17%	18%	19%	20%	21%	22%	Rate of discount 23%	24%	25%	26%	28%	30%	35%	40%	45%	50%
1	0.855	0.847	0.840	0.833	0.826	0.820	0.813	0.806	0.800	0.794	0.781	0.769	0.741	0.714	0.690	0.667
2	1.585	1.566	1.547	1.528	1.509	1.492	1.474	1.457	1.440	1.424	1.392	1.361	1.289	1.224	1.165	1.111
3	2.210	2.174	2.140	2.106	2.074	2.042	2.011	1.981	1.952	1.923	1.868	1.816	1.696	1.589	1.493	1.407
4	2.743	2.690	2.639	2.589	2.540	2.494	2.448	2.404	2.362	2.320	2.241	2.166	1.997	1.849	1.720	1.605
5	3.199	3.127	3.058	2.991	2.926	2.864	2.803	2.745	2.689	2.635	2.532	2.436	2.220	2.035	1.876	1.737
6	3.589	3.498	3.410	3.326	3.245	3.167	3.092	3.020	2.951	2.885	2.759	2.643	2.385	2.168	1.983	1.824
7	3.922	3.812	3.706	3.605	3.508	3.416	3.327	3.242	3.161	3.083	2.937	2.802	2.508	2.263	2.057	1.883
8	4.207	4.078	3.954	3.837	3.726	3.619	3.518	3.421	3.329	3.241	3.076	2.925	2.598	2.331	2.109	1.922
9	4.451	4.303	4.163	4.031	3.905	3.786	3.673	3.566	3.463	3.366	3.184	3.019	2.665	2.379	2.144	1.948
10	4.659	4.494	4.339	4.192	4.054	3.923	3.799	3.682	3.571	3.465	3.269	3.092	2.715	2.414	2.168	1.965
11	4.836	4.656	4.486	4.327	4.177	4.035	3.902	3.776	3.656	3.543	3.335	3.147	2.752	2.438	2.185	1.977
12	4.988	4.793	4.611	4.439	4.278	4.127	3.985	3.851	3.725	3.606	3.387	3.190	2.779	2.456	2.196	1.985
13	5.118	4.910	4.715	4.533	4.362	4.203	4.053	3.912	3.780	3.656	3.427	3.223	2.799	2.469	2.204	1.990
14	5.229	5.008	4.802	4.611	4.432	4.265	4.108	3.962	3.824	3.695	3.459	3.249	2.814	2.478	2.210	1.993
15	5.324	5.092	4.876	4.675	4.489	4.315	4.153	4.001	3.859	3.726	3.483	3.268	2.825	2.484	2.214	1.995
16	5.405	5.162	4.938	4.730	4.536	4.357	4.189	4.033	3.887	3.751	3.503	3.283	2.834	2.489	2.216	1.997
17	5.475	5.222	4.990	4.775	4.576	4.391	4.219	4.059	3.910	3.771	3.518	3.295	2.840	2.492	2.218	1.998
18	5.534	5.273	5.033	4.812	4.608	4.419	4.243	4.080	3.928	3.786	3.529	3.304	2.844	2.494	2.219	1.999
19	5.584	5.316	5.070	4.843	4.635	4.442	4.263	4.097	3.942	3.799	3.539	3.311	2.848	2.496	2.220	1.999
20	5.628	5.353	5.101	4.870	4.657	4.460	4.279	4.110	3.954	3.808	3.546	3.316	2.850	2.497	2.221	1.999

I *Index*

Tackling Coursework

Projects, Assignments, Reports and Presentations

David Parker

This book provides the student with practical guidance on how to approach the coursework requirement of a typical business studies course, i.e. projects, assignments, reports and presentations. The text makes clear the different approaches needed for the different types of coursework, with examples of each in an Appendix, and there is advice on how to conduct research, collect information and present results, in either written or verbal form. It is expected to be used on the following courses: any business studies course at undergraduate (e.g. BABS) or postgraduate (e.g. MBA) level. It would also be useful as a preparatory text for a research degree.

Contents

Introduction, Dissertations and projects, Essays and papers, Management reports, Seminars and presentations, Research methods. **Appendices:** *Further reading, Example of a dissertation proposal, Example of citations, Dissertation contents, Example of an essay.*

1st edition • 96 pp • 215 x 135 mm • 1994 • ISBN 1 85805 101 0